P. J Maitland

Diary of a Journey from Jacobabad to Panjgur

And Exploration of Eastern Mekran, 1881-82

P. J Maitland

Diary of a Journey from Jacobabad to Panjgur
And Exploration of Eastern Mekran, 1881-82

ISBN/EAN: 9783744756426

Printed in Europe, USA, Canada, Australia, Japan

Cover: Foto ©Andreas Hilbeck / pixelio.de

More available books at **www.hansebooks.com**

DIARY

OF A

JOURNEY FROM JACOBABAD TO PANJGUR,

AND

EXPLORATION OF EASTERN MEKRAN.

1881-82.

BY

CAPTAIN P. J. MAITLAND,
DEPUTY ASSISTANT QUARTER MASTER GENERAL, INTELLIGENCE BRANCH.

SIMLA:
GOVERNMENT CENTRAL BRANCH PRESS.
1883.

SIMLA;
PRINTED AT THE GOVERNMENT CENTRAL BRANCH PRESS.

DIARY OF A JOURNEY
FROM
JACOBABAD TO PANJGUR
AND
EXPLORATION OF EASTERN MEKRAN.

By Captain P. J. MAITLAND, Dy. Ast. Qr. Mr. Genl., Intelligence Branch.

1881-82.

Sunday, 20th November.—JACOBABAD TO CHAJERA. 15 miles. Take Mowladad road past Railway station. Mowladad 6½ miles. Very heavy road. Most bridges broken. Country quite flat and partially cultivated, otherwise thin jungle. Practicable for artillery. Chájera a short distance off road to left.

Monday, 21st November.—KAIRA GARHI. 19 miles. Bigári Bridge, (very good of brick), 3 miles. Then south to Dodapur 4 miles, (7 miles). Road along Bigári bank is not practicable for carts, and the bank is broken; baggage on mules went along it all right. It saves about 3 miles in distance but not much in time. From Dodapur west to Kaira Garhi. 12 miles. Good brick bridge over Bigári. On further side ½ mile of water to village; firm bottom, but still too deep for baggage animals with loads. Shallow places here and there caused boat to stick, and we made 4 trips, taking 4 hours to get all across. Road not nearly so heavy. Country as before.

Tuesday, 22nd November.—Halted; shooting in jheel. Very extensive. It is on right (north) side of canal. Nearly a mile across, and stretches from some way above Kaira Garhi to many miles below. Has only been so large of late years. Village of Kaira Garhi now almost deserted, some of the people having gone to Allahabad, but most to Nowa Deyra, north-west beyond the jheel. Kaira Garhi post long discontinued. Camp ground for a large force will be south of Bigári, for detachment or single battalion the green by the village if dry.

Wednesday, 23rd November.—Halted; hoping to get in perambulator sent back from Chajera. Shooting.

Thursday, 24th November.—GANDAKA. 16 miles. North-north-west across jheel. Mules and ponies carried their loads all right, good sandy bottom. At 4½ miles cross boundary Kalát and British territory. At about 2½ miles, tomb of Nawab Khan, Gadhi Baluch, said to be several hundred years old. It is small, of brick plastered white, and is in good preservation. At 4 miles Nowa Garhi, a bran new village, people from Kaira Garhi. Zamindars Mir Ghulam Mahomed and Shah Ali, Jamali Baluchis. Thence turn at right angles to left (south-west) through open country with a good deal of cultivation (high jowari), to Piara Jamali about 3 miles from Nowa Garhi. Then south to Jang Dost Jamali 2½ miles (total 10 miles from Kaira Garhi). On, southwards and westwards, winding about a great deal to find bridges over numerous small canals: country is quite flat, open, and well cultivated. The jowari now being cut.

All this being watered from the *Sirwah* canal (continuation of Bigari) half the revenue goes to Government; the other half to the Khan. There are some water wheels. At 13 miles hamlet of Dildar Jamáli. Thence about 3 miles to Gandaka, first south-west and then south-east.

Friday, 25th November.—Halted. Shooting. Gandaka is a fair sized village on slightly raised ground at the edge of the jheel, which terminates about a mile below. There is a bridge here over the Sirwah. Banks of canal to Kaira Garhi are said to be too broken on both sides for riding. Seems strange the left bank should be impracticable. This place is said to be so called from having been destroyed by an earthquake in ancient times. The Zamíndar is Shah Khan Jamali. Jamalis altogether 2,500 men; half in British territory. Chief is Din Mahomed of Roján.

Saturday, 26th November.—Still halted waiting for camel and perambulator. Both came in about noon. Bought a mare.

Sunday, 27th November.—KITCHI. 26 miles. Elevation about 865 feet. Marched at 9-30, but did not get in till 6, owing to missing the road several times, and we must have covered over 30 miles. From Gandaka, cultivation extends westwards 5 or 6 miles (in places 10 miles); then a strip of desert about 10 miles across; beyond this enter cultivated country of Magzi Baluch watered by karezes and hill streams. Shádihar, marked by a group of good sized trees, is 20 miles, but water there was reported very scanty. We left it about 1½ miles to our left and passed on to Kitchi; country jungly where not cultivated, and is like Jacobabad district, except for back ground of hills. There are numerous "jugas" scattered about, and a good deal of cultivation. Population all Magzis and Kosahs, except a few bunnias (bakhal) in each village. Magzis muster 4,000. Chief Kaisar Khan, a young man, lives at Tal. Ill-feeling between Magzis and Rinds still exists, but Kaisar Khan, Sirdar Khan, (the young chief of the Rinds) and Hasad Khan, Sarawan Sirdar, are all related by marriage and act together. The Kosahs are over 1,000 under Mánik Khan. They act with the Magzis. The Rinds are said to be 8,000. Kitchi is a good sized place, but scattered: there are bunnias here, and supplies fairly plentiful, though dear. Hills about 2½ miles off.

Passed to-day, at about four miles, and again further on, roads leading to Dár. At about 8 miles, 4 small trees on right; these are a land mark. Jowari fields on left. There was no defined road at all to Shádihar. Beyond that are wide tracks to Kitchi, Bárija, &c. In the cultivated country on either side of the desert artillery can march, but would be much restricted in manœuvring from irrigation cuts. Cavalry too would be somewhat hampered.

For about 13 miles in the middle of this march there is no water. No apparent way of shortening the stage, unless Shádihar water-supply (a few cutcha wells) could be improved. Being near the hills rain falls in this country and assists cultivation.

Monday, 28th.—Halted.

People left behind came straggling in up to 10 o'clock.

According to everybody's story there is no road to Nar or any other point in the Mula. The road goes to *Kark* (Koork on map) thence to Zidí. (See Route No. 1.)

From Kitchi to Shádádpur is 32 miles. The Sirwah is crossed half way, and would be convenient to halt at. Village of Bahram 8 miles from Shádádpur.

Jal is 20 miles from Kitchi.

In the evening rode to Báríja, a short 3 miles. At 2 miles pass small village of Mánik Khan Kosah, a friend of Kaisar Khan, who keeps his mares here.

Báríja is exactly opposite Láka Pír glen. The turning into the hills at Súnt (this word seems to mean *end* or *termination*:—here of the outer range) is north-north-west, apparently about 9 miles distant, *i. e.*, 12 from Kitchi. To north are no hills, but a lot of low jungle amidst which is said to be cultivation. The Mula water flows outside, and beyond that Bolan water is said to come down. Súnt water forms the channel between Shádihar and Kitchi. People here expect rain in winter, and depend on it to a certain extent for their crops. Many camels are bred in this country.

The pass called Pír Gájí-ka-lak or simply Kand, is about due west of Báríja. It is on the second range. The village of Báríja is nothing more than two or three adjacent hamlets of fakirs.

Tuesday, 29*th*.—ALKAH (HAJI MARI KUBAH). 11½ miles. South by east parallel to hills. At about 1 mile village of Mitah. Wahdera* Ali Morad Magzi. Beyond this the country is quite open, and there is little cultivation near the road. At about 5 miles is a solitary tree, 100 yards from which a scarcely perceptible trench marks the British boundary; placed on the map at about 6 miles. Westward it goes to Pír Surk, a ziarat at foot of hills, and on the top of the big hill *Kadaháni* (Kadaháni is a Magzi hamlet) is said to be a cairn erected as a boundary mark by our surveyors. Eastward, the line goes right away across the pat. It also marks the division between Magzis and Chándias.

The hills here are inhabited by a section of Maris called *Badáni*. Their chief is Jín Khan, and they number about 100 to 150 men. They are quite unlike the main body of the tribe and are called fakirs by the Magzis, *i. e.*, very poor inoffensive people: they are pastoral.

At about 12 miles is a mound covered with broken pottery and called Mehar. About 2 miles to right front from this, (*i. e.*, south) is a large white tomb on a low hill. This is Haji Mari Kubah. Beyond the tomb, to south-west, is a sort of hollow or valley, almost surrounded by low hills. Here are 4 groups of wells within a radius, from the centre of the valley, of about half a mile. They have distinctive names. That to east is Barah (1), to south Alkáh (2), to south-west Durb (3), to west Drabáni (4): 1 and 2 are nearest to the road: 3 is the best water, then 4, then 2. No. 1 (Barah) is decidedly brackish. Alkáh has one big well of fair water, and some small ones. Altogether water for 2 or 3 battalions with their baggage. The valley is grown with low jungle and small trees. Firewood and camel grazing abundant, kirbee is procurable within a few miles. All other supplies must be carried. Soil here is soft, deep sand.

The road as far as Mehar mound is good and well defined. Beyond, various tracks diverge, but Haji Mari Kubah is a land mark that cannot be missed.

Wednesday, 30*th*.—GHAIBI DEYRA WELLS. 15¼ miles. Eastwards to gain main track, which is, however, not very clear. Then south-south-east; country open, low hills to right gradually diverging. Low jungle, and very little cultivation visible. At 1½ miles pass Durb, a Chándia hamlet on the Durb Nai, about 2 miles off towards the hills. At 12½ miles pass tombs on the right. At 13½ miles turn to left (the village of Ghaibi Deyra is visible about 2 miles straight on). Hence through high open jungle of " kalel." At 15¼ miles reach wells containing abundant supply of good water. The water at Ghaibi Deyra itself

* Wadhera is a term applied by some tribes to their Chiefs.

is salt and very inferior. The people of the village get their drinking water from here.

Close to are some dozen huts and "jugas." The jungle is quite open enough for camping. Country about here subject to hill floods.

Village of Ghaibi Deyra about 1½ miles south-west. It is a good sized place containing residence of Ghaibi Khan, chief of the Chándias, and now an old man. No cultivation near: about 30 bunnias' shops in the village, and supplies procurable in neighbourhood; but in case of a large force, previous arrangement should be made through Shikárpur and Larkana civil authorities.

Thursday, 1st December. Halted. A great deal of difficulty in getting information about roads. It seems the old road from here by which officers used to go to Daryaro is blocked by land slips. These are of frequent occurrence, and the road wants renewing every year. It is now impassable for any animal, (See Route No. 11). A road from Pír Godra by the Arbáb Lak is however reported open and used by kafilas. Have heard of this, and as it has never been explored, determined to try it. However, I have got so much further to the south than was contemplated, that it is necessary to go into Larkána, and have a look at the roads leading from thence westwards. Ordered people to Hamal, and prepared to start very light.

Friday, 2nd December.—KAMBAR. 21 miles. From camp south-east through open jungle for about 1¼ miles to main road; here a rough cart track leading straight to Ghaibi Deyra village.

Turn east down road, which soon improves. It is an ordinary unmetalled district road cut straight across country.

At 9 miles cross road from Shádádpúr to Hamal. Shádádpúr is said to be 8 kos. Beyond this the road is narrow, trenched on either side, and the country shows signs of being within the annual inundation of the Indus. Cultivation begins to appear. Otherwise low jungle.

At 12 miles on left (north) of road is the village of Shaik Nur Mahomad Sindi.

At 13 miles Mian, or Mihan, Káhi (Dost Mahomed Khan—Burdi Baluch) a good sized village with 10 or 12 bunnias' shops: 2 paka wells, one north, one south of village, a third some distance north; water abundant, 12 feet from surface. Rice is principal kharif crop here. Jowari and wheat, rabi crops.

Owing to inundation, road is generally impassable from June till October, but would be always fit for troops in December.

Good ground for camping, west and north of village, according to crops.

Hence to Kambar bungalow, 8 miles; unmetalled road quite straight, and very good; country more wooded and cultivated. It is subject to inundation. 4 small irrigation canals; 2 unbridged. One wants some cutting down for guns.

Kambar is a small town with bazar, &c., the head-quarter of a taluka in the Larkána district of the Shikárpur Collectorate. Water abundant, and exists everywhere a few feet below surface. Camping ground had better be selected when required. Supplies abundant.

Saturday, 3rd December.—LARKANA. 12 miles. From bungalow east, road (unmetalled) narrow and raised, with ditch on either hand all the way. Trees along it give complete shade as far as the Sirkari Wah, 3 miles. This is crossed by a high pitched brick bridge. Several other and smaller canals have all good paka brick bridges, except two near Larkána, the bridges of which are katcha, as also some culverts. Road very good, except last 3 miles, which is heavy in sand, this piece is much broader than the first.

Country, annually inundated, is well wooded with lines of large babul along canal banks, &c. Soil, a rather stiff clay, is rich, and on the whole well cultivated. Staple grains are: karif—rice; and rabi—wheat and jowari. Some gram is also grown. Many villages Although last flood was below average, a good deal of water is still out. Troops must keep to roads in marching, but infantry and cavalry could manœuvre.

At 10 miles cross Gár, a large semi-natural channel. Good brick bridge. Thence road turns south-east. Railway Station, south of town, is 12 miles.

Left this evening for Jacobabad.

Sunday, 4th December.—In Jacobabad.

Monday, 5th December.—To Bádra (the second station below Larkána), 7 hours by rail. Thence to Nasírabád, 7½ miles.

Road leads away west from the station, and at 1 mile turns to right to gain Bádra village. Passing west of this it goes straight to Nasírabád. Unmetalled district road, heavy in some places. Country partly cultivated, partly low jungle. After 3 miles from Bádra there is a shallow ditch on either road side. A bungalow at Nasírabád. Water abundant. Supplies ditto.

Tuesday, 6th December.—HAMAL. 20 miles. From Nasírabad west to Gájí Kohava. Unmetalled district road, slightly raised and with ditches. A large unbridged canal close to Nasírabád. Country mostly jungle. Just before reaching Gájí cross Wárah—Mehar road: former 6 miles north, latter 8 miles south. Zamindar of Gájí is Lánah Sindi: 20 bunnias: 4 kutcha wells, with not much water; but a good deal more might be got by digging a number of wells. However, cavalry and artillery might go by Wárah to Hamal. Low tamarisk jungle all round Gájí. Hence on, nearly straight, to Gáhí Chándia, 11 miles. Country and road pretty much as before; no villages near road, but several visible at a distance. Irrigation cuts have only stick bridges, and would have to be cut down for guns; but almost any canal in the country can be thus made passable by the men of a battery in 10 minutes to half an hour.

At Gáhí is one good cutcha well to east of village; and 2 miles before reaching the same, on the right hand (north) side of the road from Gájí, is a paka well. The Zamindar of Gáhí is Ali Baksh Chándia. There are 15 bunnias' shops. Camping ground west according to cultivation. To east all is low jungle.

Hamal is 2 miles north of Gáhí on main south road through Ghaibi Dera to Máhdeh, whence I believe it joins the main road to Karachi. Máhdeh is 7 koss from Gájí. Hamal is a good sized village, Wahdera Mirza Khan Chándia. There are 20 bunnias' shops. To south-east of village is a good paka well, with plenty of water about 22 feet below surface, quality good: it is raised by a coorla worked by a bullock or by hand. Good deal of cultivation here.

Wednesday, 7th December.—PIR GODRA hamlet. About 10 miles from Hamal by direct road; 10½ by Gáhí (8½ from Gáhí itself).

First to Gáhí. Thence south-west towards low hills, country quite open, cultivated here and there. Road is a well defined cart track. At 6 miles (from Gáhí) enter hills by a gap. On left hand of entrance are two paka graves, one of Masino Rind, by whose name the gap is known. The outer range is conglomerate, and does not rise to more than about 250 feet above plain. Within are still lower parallel ridges of dark coarse sand stone or sand shale. The gap through first ridge is very short; thence road turns south-south-west, between ridges, for one mile, crossing a water shed. When nearly opposite end of conglomerate ridge, it turns again to right through a small "lak," on the further side of which is Pir Gódra tomb, and a few huts (7½ miles). The cart road goes round to south. About ½ a mile south-west of the tomb is a cutcha well with not much water.

The tract now entered is a sort of sandy valley well grown with trees and bushes. It is about 1½ miles across.

The road goes on nearly west, and crosses the Dilah, a very broad, shallow, dry channel. Here is ¾ of a mile of deep sand.

On further bank of Dilah are more huts and some patches of cultivation (8¼ miles from Gáhí). Camp here; water from 2 cutcha wells in bed of nala; 12 feet to water and 4 or 5 feet of latter. It is excellent, and abundance might be got by digging more wells.

People here and at the "Shah" (Pir's tomb) are Chándia Balúch; 1 bunnia at the Shah.

Direct road from Hamal crosses low hills north of Pir Godralak. Distance from Hamal 10 miles.

Thursday, 8th December.—KALIANI. 11 miles. North-west for a mile, then bend left and ascend Sagro, a shallow, dry, sandy water-course joining Dilah. It is about 500 yards wide, low sandstone elevations on either side the bed, which contains scattered jungle.

At 3½ miles quit Sagro, which comes from south-west. Track also bends leftwards and traverses an open stony plain, diagonally, towards the next range of low hills. This plain is about 3 mile wide, and of great length from north-north-east, to south-south-west. It is called Firáj to north and Lúndo to south. Small trees and bushes are pretty thickly scattered over it. At about 8 miles reach a gap in conglomerate ridge through which escapes the Kadari Nala to join the Sagro. Descent into Kadari is rough, with loose stones. Fair camel track, and could easily be made all right for guns.

Hence rough road up Kadari, passing through ridge and over a small stony plateau, beyond which is another descent into nala.

Road continues up Kadari in a westerly direction. It is rough, but not difficult for camels. Hills on either side close in but are of no great height.

After some distance (at 10½ miles) there is a sharp turn to the right, following the torrent; here the jungle almost disappears, and naked hills enclose a narrow barren valley. After half a mile a turn to the left is made to pass through a small ridge; thence nala bed again bends to right (north).

At the corner, however, is the camping ground. It is sandy and confined. On a small stony plateau to right (east) a little more room might be found, but altogether a single battalion would be rather crowded. Water from two holes in bed of torrent. These are springs, but very small ones. People of the country (Chándias) say that 200 sowars would always find water, at least up to the hot weather; but one would not think so to see the spot. About 1½ miles higher up there is said to be a better watering place, however this is right off the road.

There is a little coarse grass on the hills, but even mules will hardly eat it. Wood abundant, and camel forage tolerable. No supplies or permanent inhabitants.

Friday, 9th December.—ARBAB. 12¼ miles. From camp southwards, crossing nala, and entering a small defile between sandstone rocks. Then a small open space succeeded by a steep and rather rough descent to Karara nala. Camel track fair up to this point. Path turning to right (west) ascends Karara. A short distance up is brackish water, and a little short grass on right hand side. Place called Táfúi. Táfú is a flat stone for baking bread. There are many places so called, at, or near, points where hill routes enter the plains. Here the nomad Brahuis going down for the cold weather select the táfás which are to serve them till they return to the hills in spring. General direction south-south-west; road tolerable for camels. At 1¾ miles turn to south-west. All along the road has been more or less of a defile, and the hills now begin to get higher and close in on the nala. At 2½ miles some very rough places. The hills are now high, and defile narrowing. At 3 miles enter a gorge with entrance only about 10 feet. Further on the rocks fall back somewhat, but there are many very narrow places. The ascent is considerable, and road bad, over fallen blocks and boulders. Loaden camels can only just get along. Even riding is difficult. This defile pierces the considerable ridge, visible from the plain, between the low outer hills and the main range. The enclosing heights are lofty and precipitous. At two points the defile forks, in the first instance rather deceptively, but the right hand branch is to be kept to in both instances.

At about 4½ miles, quit torrent bed for the hill side to left; ascent good; descent steep, but a fair camel track. At 5 miles regain nala. Road still very rough and bad.

At about 6 miles, quit torrent and pass over a low kotal, camel track good. (Rise from Kaliani 78 feet in a mile).

After a slight descent road continues up another ravine. Rough but better.

At about 7½ miles turn to left and cross a third kotal, this is a watershed. Thence down a ravine, narrow and rather winding, general direction south-west. There are some rough places, but road tolerable, and easier as one advances.

At 10 miles reach the Arbáb Nai, and turn up it. It is a big, wooded ravine, containing a cheerful stream rippling through boulders, with occasional deepish pools. Average breadth when in one channel about 20 feet. After 1½ mile there is cultivation, a long strip on right bank. At 12 miles the valley forks. That from the left contains the Pir Láka* Nai which does not come from very far. To the right is the Arbáb. There is more cultivation about the fork, and the banks of both streams are thickly wooded with babul, tamarisk, &c.

People hereabouts are Sasúli Bráhúis, called *Laki*, from living near the "lak" (pass). It is however Chándia country of Mir Mahomed's section. The Wahdera of Arbáb is Faiz Mahomed Chándia. Two Sind policemen are stationed here.

A considerable force might camp on the cultivated land if clear of crops. There is little or no room elsewhere. Wood, water and camel grazing abundant and good. Some natural grass is also procurable.

This road is evidently much used. A wool kafila of about 16 camels is

---

* The same as be of the hot spring. There are several spots called after Pir Laka, who was a very peripatetic saint.

here. People are of Gáj, but goods belong to traders of Karak and Zidi. Horsemen took 5¼ hours to do the march. Mules light laden 6½ hours. Camels 11 hours.

The hills around abound with gad (oorial) and ibex. They are sometimes visited by officers in search of sport.

Saturday, 10th December.—BÁPRI. 11 miles. Up Arbáb for about 2 miles, rather rough but nothing very bad. Here the head of the stream is formed by two ravines. No water from this point to camp. Track now leads diagonally up a smooth bare rock slope. It is very slippery in places, and shod horses can hardly get along. Camels do better. This ascent, about ¾ of a mile in length, is the worst bit of the road, but a good path might easily be made, similar to that on the north side of Chappar.

Above the ascent is a stony level space, or small plateau. On the left is a deep ravine coming abruptly to an end.

At 3½ miles' track again begins to ascend, and winds along stony hill sides, rising steadily. The gradients are easy, and the path a tolerable one for camels.

At about 5 miles there is a descent, but it is not a long one. In the next mile are several rough places, obliging horsemen to dismount. Here, as elsewhere, the great difficulty is the slipperiness of the limestone boulders, polished by much traffic.

After this the road is fairly rideable, though not good.

At about 8½ miles reach, and cross, the shoulder of a spur which projects from the lowest part of the main range near where the road crosses it. Two patches of cultivation some way off on the slopes of the main ridge are called Kubi and belong to Sásúlis. No water.

Hence bend to left (south-west) along the slopes of the spur above mentioned; a ravine on the right divides it from the main range.

At 11 miles reach camping ground opposite a big hole of good water in the ravine below. Ground very confined, and it is difficult to say where more could be found. There might be a place cleared some way up the hill side to east.

Everywhere the hill sides have a thin sprinkling of small trees and bushes. The ravines are thickly grown.

It is evident that this road has at some time or other been regularly made as a camel track, and this is said to have been done by the Tálpurs. It sadly wants re-making however. There are no great natural difficulties. The gradients are easy, and it is only necessary to clear away the blocks of limestone which in places strew the hill side, to fill up the spaces between them with rubble, and level the path over it.

Mules (light laden) took 6 hours to do the march. Camels 9½ hours. However, one of the latter fell and died of internal injuries.

Wood and water abundant at Bápri, but no camel grazing.

Froze in the night.

Sunday, 11th December.—GAJ. 8¼ miles. From camp about ¾ of a mile to crest of main range, road fair. Ascent of last bit is rather steep but easy. Good view from crest over a rocky country, more open however than that between the foot of the range and the Sind plain. A white limestone hill bearing 292½ true, is Pinju. At the foot of this, on the further side, is the camping ground so called, rather more than half way to Zidí from Gáj. Elevation of crest 4,500 feet.

The name Káro is sometimes applied to the whole range.

On the west side there is a scarp along the ridge: in some places it is 200 feet high or more. The road passes at lowest point. Below the scarp on the further side is a "tal" or basin about ¾ of a mile long, by 250 yards across. It is cultivated, but there is no permanent water. Its name is Búchi.

To this is an abrupt drop of 150 feet. The roads zigzags down it, and is rough, with one bad slippery place.

Crossing the tal, again descend by a rough winding track. The slopes are much steeper and more broken on this side of the hill than on the east.

At about 2 miles from the crest (2¾ miles from camp) pass water, at the head of a ravine. After this the track is rather better, but still not good.

At about 6 miles reach the bottom of the hill, and turn down a broad wooded ravine.

Two miles of this brings into the Saonar valley, about ½ a mile wide, and almost filled by the shingly bed of the torrent, which is thickly grown with large tamarisk, &c. Water only in pools. It is drawn away in some places to irrigate patches of cultivation.

Crossing Saonar, the hamlet of Gáj is found under the low hills opposite. It consists of some half dozen huts and a bunnia's shop. Camp on a small piece of cultivated land. Wood, water and camel grazing abundant. A little bhoosa, grain and ata. Also some coarse grass. The people are Sasúlí Bráhúis.

A short distance below (south), the Saonar unites with the Bhinní to form the Gáj river, which then flows away south through a narrow valley. It is a perennial stream.

There is ample ground for encampment about a mile north of the hamlet, on the same side the Saonar. Here is a little cultivated land.

Monday, 12th December.—Halted. Trying to change camels, but could get none. Surveying all day.

Froze here harder than at Bápri, but still not much.

Tuesday, 13th December.-PARELO. 13 miles. Mahomed Ali Sasúlí, wahdera of Gáj, reports many robbers on the pass. There are both Sasúlís and Chándias, as well as some others. They plunder single travellers, or small unarmed parties, and also lift cattle. Up to the time of Nasir Khan Hud of Kalát, the local Sásúlí chief had charge of the pass, and I understand received an allowance from the Kalát treasury to keep up men. But since the British boundary was drawn along the crest of the range this has been discontinued, and the road is now unprotected, and somewhat unsafe. This together with the track having now got so much out of repair, greatly militates against the road being used as a trade route. It is by far the shortest road from Central Baluchistan to the railway at Lárkána, &c., and such trade as there is (including that of Panjgúr) would come this way, if the road was made good and safe. Mahomed Ali petitions that the allowance may be restored, and is willing to be responsible for the safety of the pass. The robbers are said to take refuge in British territory.

From Gáj hamlet, through low ranges, more or less parallel, in a westerly direction, afterwards inclining to south-west; road open and good. At about 4 miles enter the Rehi or Bhinní, a broad and shallow torrent, here four or five hundred yards across. Its stony bed is quite dry, and thickly grown with tamarisk.

The track keeps to the right hand edge (left bank) of the Rehi for several miles. It then crosses, and passes inside of an outer ridge of hills, keeping parallel to the course of the torrent. These hills are joined on to a rather higher range on the left hand side.

Ascending here, the road winds among hills, over stony slopes, for half a mile or more. At 10 miles the crest is reached, and then, turning to the left, there is a rough descent through a narrow gap. At 11 miles is a little water in a nala. It is called Ashkáni. There is room to camp within a few hundred yards. A very hilly country is now entered. The ranges are steep, but of no great height and have a general arrangement in parallel lines, which is however only observeable when they are overlooked from a considerable elevation. Between them are narrow ravines, and the track passes from one of these to another, generally descending, but with an occasional ascent. All the ravines are full of palmetto scrub (písh), and are sprinkled with bushes. The hills are bare, and appear here to be trap, or a very dark coloured, fine grained, sandstone. The higher ranges are, like Káro, of grey limestone.

The last 500 yards into camp is through a narrow gap, up the rocky bed of a nala containing water, and the path is rough and difficult.

With this exception, and a few yards in descending from the kand crossed at 10 miles, the road is a very fair camel track all the way.

There is room for a small body of troops to encamp. Wood and water abundant, camel grazing tolerable: some coarse grass in the hills.

Did not freeze last night owing, no doubt, to sheltered position.*

NOTE.—*Parelo.* On the hill overlooking the water to south are some small sangars. These were put up by the Sásúlís on the occasion of a great Chándia raid in the time of Wali Mahomed father of Ghaibi Khán. It seems the Sásúlís had a quarrel with the Gahicho Balúch, allies, or dependants, of the Cháudias, the former being the aggressors. The feud spread until Wali Mahomed himself took the field at the head of his clan and inflicted great loss on the Sásúlís. There is no enmity now-a-days.

Wednesday, 11th December.—PINJU, 5¼ miles. This was a mistake; the distance being represented as only a little less than yesterday.

From camp, instead of keeping on up the nala (west-north-west) turn to the left up a ravine, between the hill where the sangars are, and the white ridge in front. This is going back: slight ascent for ¼ a mile. Descent rather steeper. Then turn to the right, through a gap, and again to the right, going along between the white ridge on the right, and a dark ridge on the left. At about 2¼ miles pass gap in the former, which would seem to be the natural outlet for the road from camp, and if the track were taken through here it would save at least a mile.

On through the hills, road fairly open, and good all the way.

At 4 miles strike the Koláchí nala. In general characteristics it resembles the Saonar and Rebi, but is not so wide, and contains a small perennial stream. It flows to the Gáj, but does not join it for about 35 miles. The greater part of its course is through narrow defiles. Track turns up Koláchí. On the left bank is cultivation about 1000 yards long. The place is called Chárnárch. It is about 17 miles from Gáj (which might be made 16 see above). Wood, water and camel grazing abundant. A little bhoosa is procurable, and also natural grass; the latter is indifferent stuff, but much better than nothing. Chárnárch would make a good halting place.

Beyond it is another piece of cultivation of about the same size called Pinju.

---

* Parelo is about 560 feet higher than Gáj hamlet.

It lies immediately under the great limestone rock Házárbuzí, which is a landmark along the whole route from the crest of the main range.

These two places would afford ample accommodation for troops at any time of year. There are no people living immediately on the spot, but about 25 to 30 families of Sásúlis are in the neighbourhood in summer, and 3 in winter. Chief man Khair Mahomed. Rice and jowari are cultivated; also wheat or a little barley as rabi crop.

Beyond the Koláchi, but at some distance, is a limestone range called Pitákh stretching a long way back,* and like Pinju, visible all over the country. At its base is the Singhán stream, said to contain a good deal of water. It joins the Koláchi.

*Thursday, 15th December.—*ZIDI. 17 miles. Straight up the Koláchi all the way, through a defile between limestone ranges, averaging a quarter of a mile in width. The tamarisk grows plentifully, and there is also a good deal of high grass: the running stream is larger than at Pinju. It is crossed frequently, quite a dozen times in the course of the march, but is very shallow.

At 5 miles, on the left bank (east side), is a patch of cultivation called Pátí.

At 6¼ (say 7½ from Chárnáreh) is more cultivation called Lakúr. Here there is room to camp; wood, water and camel grazing abundant. Exactly opposite is the big rock called Bájíai. Above this small pieces of cultivated ground on either side of the defile are pretty frequent.

At 9¼ miles, on the right bank (west side) is cultivation, and a few mulberry trees, called Kátaghar.

At about 12¼ miles the limestone ranges show signs of coming to an end. Low hills appear in front, and beyond them are plainly visible the high rocks on the further side of the Zidí valley.

At 13¼ miles cross a low spur from the hills on the right. The Koláchi, after a short twist to the left, makes a bend to the right, or rather comes from that direction.

In another mile the hills have altogether receded, and the plain opens out. The Koláchi here shows a very stony bed, over which the water trickles in various channels. Tamarisk disappears.

At 17 miles reach Zidí. Cultivation, and groups of huts, on both sides of the stream. The country is now fairly open, but the valley of Zidí, with the hamlets of Zidí proper, is beyond detached low hills in advance. Camped south of the detached hills, on the left bank of the river bed. Elevation 3,000 feet.

In this, or lower, Zidí is the residence of Paien Khan, chief of the Sásúlis. It is a comfortable looking house near the hills, about 1,000 yards east of the stream.

There is not much cultivation, and the people complain that they have more water than is sufficient for the land. Grievously hard in this country where the reverse is almost invariably the case! Rice is cultivated, also wheat and barley, &c. Large flocks of sheep graze here, and away down to Gáj.

In Zidí there are about 100 families altogether: 40 of Sásúlís, the remainder Mingals, Bizanjaos, Zehrís, &c. The fighting strength of the Sásúlis is computed by themselves at 1,000 men, but they are spread over a large tract of country, extending from Khozdar, to the British boundary on the crest of the Káro range. East they go to Gúrú and Karak (Kúrk), and west to the Sinán, beyond which is the Kidráni country.

The following are the Sásúlí subdivisions:—
Ketchizai—The Chief's own section.
Mírsízai.
Dostízai.
Balozai.
Júnzai.
Ghar.
Sopak.
Bijarzai.
Gazízai.
Shekh.
Aljárzai—On the Koláchi. Wahdera Umed Ali.
Dodazai—About Gáj. Wahdera Mahomed Ali.

The Sásúli ghidans are not of black stuff like those of most nomadic tribes, but of reed screens or mats, the material for which is abundant in the river bed. In Jháláwán generally, mat huts are a common substitute for black tents.

Friday, 16th December. Halted.

This appears to be a mild winter. Smart frost every night, but days very pleasant, No rain as yet, though this is the season. Snow seldom lies at Zídí.

Saturday, 17th December.—KHOZDAR. 17 miles. About 16 direct from camp, and 15 from Zidi proper. Elevation 3,640 feet.

First northwards, leaving detached hills on the left. Cultivation, reed beds, and grass, up the river; also scattered groups of huts. Zídí proper consists of two hamlets in which are 3 bunnia's shops. The hamlets are situated on a mound a short distance apart, and are watered by several small streams, some artificial. There are a few mulberry and other trees. Here the plain terminates to the east in a triangular stony flat, bounded by limestone hills. At the apex is a clean gap, through which lies the road to Karak, two marches distant. It is a tolerable camel road, though bad in one place. (See route No. 1).

From Zídí proper, west-north-west over plain, at first partially cultivated, afterwards bare and stony.

Main channel of the Koláchí lies to right (south), and passes west of the detached hills. The reedy streams of Zídí proper are an affluent. Our baggage, on leaving camp, crossed the river bed at once and took a straight path over a low plateau. This road, at about 4 miles, joins that from Zídí proper.

From the latter place an irrigation channel runs by the side of the road for about 5 miles, and after that the bank of the river bed is followed, so that there is water all along this march.

At about 5 miles from Zídí hamlets, strike the river bed, here running at the base of low hills on the south side of the valley. Its left bank is thenceforward followed over undulating ground.

At about 8 miles are low hills in the plain abutting on the river bed. Before reaching these, cultivation commences along the bank of the stream, alternating with great beds of tall flags and grass. The first flats near the low hills are called Sorgaz. Two and a half miles further on (10½ miles) are hamlets on the further side called Chárbájkí. Here the people are Malik, a small clan of about 30 men attached to the Sásúlís.

Thence is 4¼ miles to Khozdár fort, over stony undulations, skirting the low lying land alongside the stream. Road good all the way.

Sunday, 18th December. Halted.

There is no town or village of Khozdár. Fort as before described.* It is in good repair. The howitzer was removed last year and only the 3 Pr. left. It is a very ancient piece, and the carriage apparently unserviceable. There is a well in the fort, about 40 or 50 feet deep, with 2½ feet of water, but filth has been thrown in it. The water is naturally good. Fort contains residence of the Naib; his deputy (the Jánishín); servants and establishment. Garrison :— about 80 of the Khan's infantry and a dozen sowars. There are 5 bunnias' shops.

Around the fort, within a mile radius, are various small hamlets aggregating about 80 houses. The population consists of 40 families of Gazkís, 20 of Kúrds, 7 or 8 Nakíl, &c. Near the Chúkokoh Kand (Baghwána road) is a hamlet of some 5 or 6 houses of Bázgirs. There are 3 blacksmiths in the Khozdar hamlets, and 4 carpenters.

The Naib's name is Itobah Khan Choto (Jamót Sindi.)

Monday, 19th December.—SAMAND. 17 miles. Elevation 3,930 feet. West-south-west up the glen which branches from the valley at its south-west corner, near the fort.

At first over stony slopes, leaving the broad, shallow, and dry nala (one of the two which unite to form the Koláchí) on the left. Steady gradual ascent. Track good.

At about 6 miles enter the cultivated plain of Firozabád. It is khushkawa land, carefully banked to catch the rain water.

Road leads along the top of the banks between the fields, keeping the south side the plain, which is altogether about 8 miles long, by 2 or 3 across, in the centre. It narrows towards each end, and is enclosed on all sides by hills of considerable height. From about the middle, a road goes northwards to Baghwána, &c.

At about 7½ miles pass the spot used as a camping-ground, and marked Firozabád in the map. It is off the road to the right. Major M. Green, Commandant, 2nd Sind Horse, in his report dated Kalát 11th June 1860, says the camping ground is good and dry ; water good and abundant, firewood procurable from bed of river. No supplies.

There is no village of Firozabád, but a few small groups of huts are scattered up and down the valley. At 8 miles pass between rocks which are outliers of a spur from the hills on the left.

At 9 miles, just to right of the road, is a well 80 feet deep, with 5 feet of good water. Within a mile of this is a narrow strip of low jungle crossed by the road and affording abundant firewood. A small detachment might conveniently encamp west of the well.

The plain of Firozabád appears to be slightly curved ; convexity to the north. The road is pretty straight, entering it near the northern hills, touching those on the south, and again after passing the well, crossing the plain to its extreme west end, where it enters the hills on the north at about 14 miles from Khozdár. Before doing so the track to Wad diverges, leading on south-south-west up the prolongation of the valley, which is here divided by a watershed,

* See my report on the Mula Pass, &c 1872

notable as the boundary between Firozabád and Nál lands, (*i. e.*, between Mingals and Bízanjaos).

Immediately after passing the first low elevation, a broad track is crossed. This is the road from Baghwána to Wad. A confused mass of low hills is now traversed, the road leading long the beds of small nalas. It is a good camel tarck, but would require a little improvement to make it fit for artillery.

At about 15 miles there is water, a few yards up a small ravine to the right. The place is marked by a huge boulder, or fallen block, on the right of the road and not easily mistaken. Here are several small springs of good water. There is no good ground to camp, but it does not appear to be worse than Samand in that respect. The spot is called Gáhéto.

Two miles more through the hills, (by which time their further side is nearly reached), brings to a water hole under a rock, which appears to contain a supply sufficient for two or three squadrons, and the people state it is seldom less than at present. However, on the 27th February 1860, Major M. Green, with a detachment of 2nd Sind Horse, found so little that he was obliged to continue his march to Nál.

Camping ground at Samand on low stony flats on left bank of the nala. About 2 battalions and 2 squadrons might find room, but with difficulty. The camping ground is commanded on all sides. Wood scanty, camel grazing ditto; no supplies or grass.

There are 4 water holes at intervals down the nala beyond the first one. The furthest is $1\frac{1}{2}$ miles. By taking advantage of all these a considerable force might encamp. The water is rather saline but quite drinkable.

After crossing the watershed, the drainage is to the south-west to the Wad valley, whence it escapes to the Puráli.

Tuesday, 20th December.—NAL. 10 miles. Elevation 3,575 feet. A bullock kafila passed camp this morning; about 15 beasts, laden with dates, from Nál for Khozdár.

On the march met a kafila of 49 camels laden with dates bound for Gandáva. At Nál was another kafila of 19 camels laden with dates from Panjgúr, and going to Gandáva and Shikárpúr by the Múla. *Yesterday* we met a kafila of 40 camels, laden with dates and wool, from Nal bound for Gandáva. Altogether the trade seems to be considerable.

Track down nala for $1\frac{1}{4}$ miles, when it quits it to the right, and passing low hills, enters undulating gravelly plateaux sloping away to the plain of Nál.

At $1\frac{3}{4}$ miles enter the hollow of the Jaori nala, which comes from the hills just quitted. At $2\frac{1}{4}$ miles leave the Jaori. Descent and ascent very easy. The plain of Nál is now fairly entered upon.

At $3\frac{3}{4}$ miles another water course, formed by the junction of the Jaori with a nala coming from the north-east.

The plain, though flat, is stony. It is very extensive, being at least 6 or 7 miles across from east to west, and of great length from north-north-east to south-south-west. On the north it is closed by hills some miles distant: to the south it appears to narrow after about 10 miles, but is open as far as the eye can reach. The hills in the direction of Wad, or rather west of that place, are very distant. A great portion of this large expanse is gravelly or stony. In the middle a sprinkling of low scrub; and towards the centre, and on the western side, small isolated tamarisk trees are thinly scattered.

At 5 miles pass a low isolated hill, close to right of the road, called Lághor Ghar.

After this some miles of alluvial soil. The land is banked, as customary in this country, to retain water. At 6¼ miles a well on right hand (north) of road, 75 feet deep.

Nál villages are near the western hills, that where the chief resides being close under the range, here quite low. He has a large house with a walled enclosure, partially defiladed on the side towards the hill, which however quite commands it. There are about 20 houses, but some are unoccupied. On the side towards the plain is a small grove of date trees, surrounded by a wall, and there are some low walled enclosures around irrigated fields watered by a spring from the hills near by.

Mir Kahira (or Kíra) Bizanjao Sirdar, is Naib of Makrán as was his father (Fakir Mahomed) before him. His seat of Government is Kej, and his son Fakir Mahomed resides at Nál and manages local affairs. Mir Mahomed Mingal, maternal uncle of the late Núrádín (with whom he was not on good terms) is closely connected by marriage ties with the Nál family and is now here.

There are some dozen bania's shops at Nál; about 40 blacksmiths in the valley, and 10 carpenters.

The trade of Panjgúr and Khárán all comes this way. It consists principally of dates, wool, and ghi. Of the former, about 800 camel loads pass through on an average during the season. A large portion of the trade goes south to Karáchi. Both traders and camel owners prefer taking this road to going to Shikarpúr and Larkána. The banias because the transit dues (súng) are excessive on the latter route, and the camel owners because their beasts are not liable to be seized by the Khan's officials.

The journey to Karáchi takes 25 days; but the dues (payable to local Chiefs) amount only to Rs. 8 on 8 maunds of wool, and other merchandise in proportion. The hire of a camel to Karachi is Rs. 16.*

The journey to Shikarpur is not more than 18 days; but the dues amount to Rs. 13 on 8 maunds of wool, and the camel hire is 20 rupees. Rs. 4-14-0 of the dues are levied at Khozdár.

The journey to Larkána by the Arbáb route is only 12 days, and the dues, including those of Khozdár, would not amount to more than Rs. 8.

There is a good deal of khushkawa cultivation at Nál, but very little permanent water. Near the Sirdar's hamlet are one spring and one small karez. Some miles lower down the valley are three springs called Tobaroh.

The southern continuation of the plain is called Hazárganji and Garók. There is a hamlet in the former, which is some 10 or 12 miles south-south-west. Garók is to its east. Hazárganji has a spring and a karez. Sheep and goats are very plentiful in this country, but there are not many camels.

The Bízanjaos can here muster 1,000 men. They formerly bore a bad character, but are now quiet and peaceful enough. The following sections are said to be represented in Nál :—

    (1).—Hamalárí (the chief.)
    (2).—Tamarárí.

(3).—Umarári.
(4).—Siahpád.
(5).—Sájadí.

The latter are of course not Bízanjaos, but they acknowledge Mír Kahíras authority.

The Bízanjaos are of Rind origin, at least the chief's family is.

Fakir Mahomed professes to be able to turn out altogether 2,500 men without much difficulty.

The tribe extends westward into Greshak (Gressia of map, &c.), which belongs to the Sájadís. They also hold a great deal of Kolwah and the country to its south.

The Mingals can muster 2,000 men. Núrúdin's son Shakar Khan (a small boy) is the chief. Mír Mahomed states that 4,000 or 5,000 men can easily be got together and that the total number of Mingals is greater.

Wednesday, 21st December.—Halted. Surveying.

Wrote to-day to Azád Khan of Khárán stating my intention of proceeding through his country to Panjúr—if he had no objection. The letter is carried by one of the Fakír Mahomad's sowars, and I have sent one of our own Baluch Guides with him. They expect to reach Khárán in four days, and returning at once with an answer (written if possible) are to meet us in Besemar about the 28th.

Thursday, 22nd December.—Halted. Surveying.

The cultivable ground in the centre of the plain is more extensive than is apparent at first sight. It is all khushkawa. The banks surrounding the fields are high. Jhow bushes grow between the fields, and trees of the same are scattered around. There are altogether about 10 hamlets in Nál, aggregating probably some 120 houses. By far the largest is that known as "the banias' village." It contains 40 houses, including 10 shops, and is about a mile east of of the Sirdar's hamlet, which contains of only 8 or 10 families of his immediate dependants. There is a third hamlet between the two. A short distance beyond the banias' village, towards the centre of the plain, is a small, rude, sarai fort called Kaori. The population of Nál is entirely Bízanjao, and to a great extent nomadic. Ghidans may be seen at nearly every hamlet. Drinking water is for the most part from wells. Supplies are no doubt always procurable for a small force, and the banias can feed large numbers, if previous notice be given. Mutton is plentiful. Wood, water, and camel grazing are abundant. The only difficulty would be for bhoosa, which is likely to be scanty, except after an unusually good harvest. Plenty of open ground for encampment, but that near the Sirdar's village is nearly all stony. There are three water mills :—

(1).—Khúrmástan by Tobaroh.
(2). An old one not far from the chief's hamlet under the hill.
(3).—Hazárganji ; this has plenty of water.

Friday, 23rd December.—Halted. Surveying.
Saturday, 24th December.—Halted. Surveying.

From Nál to Wad is 3 stages of 12 to 14 miles each—
(1).—Kolán.
(2).—Gwanak.
(3).—Wad.

There are about 30 wells in the Nál valley ; those at the upper, or north, end are deep,—80 feet or more,—but the water is found nearer the surface as the valley is followed to the southward. These wells, or at least some of them, contain an abundant supply of water.

Sunday, 25th December.—TEGÁB. 8 miles.

Road south-west over stony plain to the hills. Pass through first spur at 1½ miles. The second spur is crossed by a low kotal: descent down a small ravine, rather rough.

A plain is then entered, enclosed between the spurs of Shábshán and Kúlérí on the south, and those of Guandor, &c., on the north. It is about 4 miles across, rough and stony, and pretty thickly grown with tamarisk. The bed of the Tégáb, which crosses it, has a very ill defined channel. It is dry.

On reaching the low hills which limit the plain on the further side, the river bed is crossed. Here there is water, said to be perennial. To-day it was several yards wide and 3 to 6 inches deep. The stream sinks into the stones a short distance below, and does not reappear (except in very small pools) till Hazárganjí is reached. There it is used for irrigation, and turns a watermill.

Camped on the right bank of the Tégáb, where there is a triangular piece of cultivated land between the spurs. Major Malcolm Green, in 1860, camped on the left bank "in rather confined ground, surrounded on three sides by low rocky hills."

There are a few beds of flags and high grass near the stream.

A little bhoosa is sometimes procurable here. Wood, water and camel grazing abundant.

The Tégáb comes from the south, round the spur. A large force would probably move on, half a mile or a mile, and camp on the stream where there is land and a house belonging to Azád Khán of Khárán.

Good road to-day. Artillery on leaving Nál would go to the end of the spur and up the bed of the Tégáb. This would increase the distance by upwards of a mile.

The Tégáb water is very slightly saline.

Monday, 26th December.—GWANAK. 9 miles. Straight west across the end of the plain of Greshak (or *Greshah*: the people here have a trick of dropping the final consonant at the end of names). First half mile through tamarisk jungle; then a little bit of alluvial soil succeeded by gravelly undulations.

On the left hand, the open plain stretches south-south-west for a considerable distance. The centre is cultivated, but there is no irrigated land. Away in the plain, about 2 miles off the road, is what looks at a distance like a fort with a tower. It is the deserted hamlet of *Tégáb* belonging to one Mehrán, but he and his people now live entirely in ghidans.

This place is mentioned by Cook as being about 2 miles to right of the Gwarjak road, which diverges from that to Khárán immediately after quitting the Tégáb camping ground. It was even then (1860) "uninhabited and falling into decay." There was a well near it.

Greshak is principally inhabited by the Sajadi, or Sájeí, who are supposed to be the ancient Sagetæ. Their chief is Haiat Khan, and they are said to muster 1,500 to 2,000 men. When the Jhálawans are called out, their contingent join the Bízanjaos.

At about four miles we crossed a broad track, which is the road from Kalat, *via* Sohráb, Gidar, &c., to Greshak and Gwarjak. (The halting place called **Greshak is 13 miles from Tégáb,—Cook**).

At 6½ miles passed between the spur of a conical hill and outlying rocks: approaching this the ground gradually becomes more broken. A nala passing through the gap is crossed, and the road continues straight on in the original direction.

The hills are now closing in on both sides, and the ascent towards the range in front, visible almost ever since leaving Nál, becomes perceptible.

At about 8½ miles, after passing a hill on the left, turn off the main road to that side, and passing between small rocky hills, reach a nala, in whose bed we found small pools of water, united by a little rill. The supply is said to be constant, and to diminish very little, even in summer. The quality is about the same as that of the Tégáb.

Plenty of room for encampment on right bank, under the hill Siáh. Also on left bank above water. Ground commanded by hills, but country perfectly friendly. No habitations or supplies. No grass. Fire-wood tolerably abundant. Some camel grazing. Elevation about 3975 feet.

Road good all the way. A rather deep nala is crossed just before leaving the main road, but guns could get over it.

Tuesday, 27th December.—KODAK. (*Bijar's well.*) 6½ miles. (15 from Tégáb). Northwards, rising steadily over undulating ground for 1¼ miles to foot of pass called the Gwanak Koh Kand. Near this the main road is rejoined.

At first there is a short piece of about 1 in 12, in zigzags. Thence the track winds round the base of a high limestone rock on the left. It is mostly very good, but one bit of a few yards is rough. There are two small descents, but the rise is generally steady to the crest of the pass, which is reached at 3¼ miles, (about 12 from Tégáb).

Elevation of crest about 4350 feet: 375 feet above camping ground at Gwanak, and 775 feet above Nál.

Here the limestone ridge (Cook's red and white limestone)* has been disrupted, and the gap is filled in by a tumbled mass of blue limestone and trappoid rocks.

Descent into a small ravine is easy. Here the path forks: the left hand branch, which is the best, continues down the ravine, and then either turns west by south down the valley for Gúndáb &c.; or to the right, round the end of a low spur, to the Kodak camping ground.

The other track goes straight to Kodak, across gravel slopes, and through low hills. It is somewhat the shortest, and is a fair camel road.

The plain is entered at about 2 miles from the crest of the Kand. It is tolerably extensive, stretching north-north-east and south-south-west for a considerable distance. The hills on the opposite side are about 5 miles distant. They are high, but diminish rapidly towards the north-east, in which direction they are seen from the summit of the pass to be overtopped by other ranges as far as the eye can reach. The whole country looks very barren and desolate.

Kodak is a good sized piece of alluvial (khushkáwa) land, belonging to Lál Khán Sumalári. No one lives permanently on the spot. The people are here and there in their ghidans. There is one well, 35 to 40 feet deep, with about 3 feet of tolerable water, not quite so good as that of Gwanak. Tamarisk bushes are scattered about.

Ample room for encampment, wood and camel grazing abundant: we procured some kirbee.

---

* Apparently the same rock as that at Gharkbai in Peshin.—See Griesbach's Report on Geology of South Afghanistán (Memoirs of Geological Survey of India No. XVIII., Pt. 1).

(Major M. Green in 1860, camped amidst tamarisk jungle in bed of river. Water rather scarce from two pools.)

Road good; but one or two bits of the K and would require making for guns :—still it is a very easy pass.

Wednesday, 28th December.—SORCHIL (*in Besemar*). 18 miles. The range to west of Kodak is called Múkh. Its crest is the boundary between Azad Khan's and Kalat territory. The line of demarcation comes round eastwards across the watershed at the head of Kodak valley, and then again northwards along the hills.

Beyond Múkh is a sort of valley, drained by a torrent called Dhúléri which goes south, down Mashkai.

Lál Khán Súmalarí lives in Koras, a few miles to the south-west.* Kodak is claimed by Haiat Khan Sájadi of Greshak; Lál Khán and the Súmalánrís are, however, in possession.

There are a number of wells in Kodak, altogether 7, including the one camped at.

No. 1 is north-west by north, about $1\frac{1}{2}$ miles, near a solitary tree towards low white hills.

No. 2 is north-east by north in a ravine seen stretching up under a red and white limestone cliff. It is called Lídí.

Nos. 3, 4 and 5. Under the hills eastward. There were formerly 2 karezes here; both are now choked, but water is found in some of the upper pits on the dámán-i-koh.

No. 6, called Kálabút—"the black spur"—is about 2 miles east-south-east, under a small dark coloured hill.

The positions of these wells were pointed out by an old Lárí (Mírávi) who lives in the neighbourhood. He states that they all contain about as much water as that by which we camped.

The pools near which Major M. Green was pitched are a mile or two down the torrent, south-west.

I would appear that by dividing the troops a large force would find sufficient water at Kodak.

Leaving camp, strike north-west, and begin to rise gradually over gravel slopes. At 2 miles pass the end of the first ridge of low white hills, which are then skirted for some distance. Ascent gradual, and road good and open.

At five miles reach the watershed, broad and flat. Small detached hills lie about, one exactly on the highest point. Here the road up the valley from Jibrí and Gúndáb comes in. Hence, northwards, the drainage is to the Gázi torrent, which goes to the plain of Kháran, and the country belongs to Azád Khán.

Descent from watershed is gentle, like the ascent.

At $5\frac{3}{4}$ miles turn to left and descend the Hokár ravine between low broken hills, the termination of the western range.

There is a water hole or two here (6 miles), and kafilas occasionally halt.

The ravine soon becomes a mere shallow darah between very low undulations of conglomerate or gravel.

At about 7 miles the nala is left, the track turning up the right bank, and continuing more or less parallel to it, over undulating gravelly slopes. This may be considered the begining of Besemar valley. Gradually the direction changes to east-north-east, the are of a circle having been traversed since

* He occasionally goes into Korás for a few weeks, but his home is at Mut.

quitting the watershed. There is said to be no direct track (although the country is quite open) on account I believe of the numerous watercourses which descend from the eastern hills.

At 12½ miles, cross the broad shallow bed of a nala, pretty thickly grown with tamarisk bushes. It joins the Hokár nala a short distance below.

Thence the track leads northwards, over a bare and elevated, but fairly smooth dámán. On the left, all the ground in the centre of the valley, about the main drainage channel, is a good deal broken, and the road keeps away from this on a higher level.

At 14½ miles pass a mound ½ a mile to left of road.

At 15 miles, cross the beds of several shallow water courses, grown with tamarisk. They run together, and the whole are about ½ a mile wide. There is a second small mound near the road on the further side.

Beyond these, at about 15½ miles, is cultivation (khúshkáwa) on the left of the road.

At about 17 miles turn abruptly to left, off the main track, and follow a rather indistinct path for a mile tarougu hummocky ground with tamarisk bushes. The camping place is on the bank of a tamarisk filled nala. Water appears, and flows sluggishly for 100 yards or more; there is none above or below. It is slightly saline, whence the name :—Sór-chíl signifying salt (or brackish) nala. The water is said to be perennial. Best ground on left (west) bank. Wood, water, and camel grazing, abundant. Tolerable grass procurable. It is called *barshon* and seems identical with the "*wijh*" grass of Shoráwak. When young it is very good, but the old stuff is useless. The grass of Mal and Manútí in the Katchi plain, is very similar in appearance, but I believe not the same. No habitations or supplies.

Thursday, 2th December.—Halted. Surveying.

The Besemar valley is about 16 miles long by 4 broad. It is drained by the Gazí uala, which beyond Drúg (10 miles to the north) is joined by the Sajít, and the two form the Garók. This pursues a zigzag course, north-west through the hills, to the plain of Kháran.

At first, Besemar appears a wilderness of gravelly *dámán* and broken hillocky ground, pretty thickly grown with tamarisk. It contains, however, a good deal of cultivation. This is all dependant on rain, but the hollows are most carefully bunded, some of the banks being 5 or 6 feet high, and the most seems to be made of the cultivable soil, which is a rich light loam, closely resembling that of Peshíu.

The country hereabouts, and to the north as far as Núshkí, belongs to Rakshání Balúch. They live entirely in ghidans, and only come here to plough, sow, and reap.

Although the surface of the valley is irregular, troops of all arms could manœuvre freely, and the road through it is good and open.

As might be expected from the elevation, the cold at this season is considerable, and it freezes hard at night, but the day (if still and not cloudy) is pleasant. The gaz is all dried up, bu. láni and some of the larger tamarisk still affords camel grazing.

The valley abounds in game. Obara and ravine deer are extraordinarily plentiful. There are also sand grouse, hares, and a few ducks.

On the west are many successive ridges of dark hills. Those next the plain appears to be syenite or some trappoid rock. To north-west are what look like limestone ranges, and as usual these are high. The whole forms a mountainous belt some 15 to 20 miles thick, which sinks gradually to the plain of Kháran. I could see nothing like clay slate (eocene shales), which appears everywhere, from Toba southwards, to form the backbone of the hills dividing the elevated region from the lower country to the west.

To-day our sowars returned from Kharán with one of Azád Khán's troopers, and a letter from Náóróz Khán, eldest son of the Sirdar. The letter was civil but unsatisfactory. I was therefore obliged to give up all hope of seeing Khárán, and determined to make the best of my way to Panjgúr *viá* Gwarjak. This necessitated returning to Kodak.

From Besemar the route to Khárán is given in No. VI.

Khárán town is reported to contain about 200 houses, and is surrounded by a high and strong wall. There is no ditch. One gateway on the south side. There is no citadel except a strong tower adjacent to the Mir's residence. There are other detached towers within the walls. One well in the town.

Eight bania's shops, and a great many blacksmiths and carpenters.

Outside the town is a karez, affording a small supply of water, which is led within the town and used for drinking by the people. It also fertilizes a few fields of lucern, for the Sirdar's horses, and his orchard, which is adjacent to the walls. When Khárán was attacked by the Khan of Kalát (in 1869 ?) his force, some 5,000 or 6,000 men, camped on this karez, the upper part of which is well out of fire from the town.

About 60 horse (armed with short rifles of native manufacture) are kept up by the Sirdar. Náóróz Khan is now raising a body of the same number of foot, for whom he has breechloaders, apparently sniders.* There are two guns on the walls, but the largest is only a 3 or 4 pounder.

There is severe drought in Khárán now. Grain is being imported, as the crops have entirely failed. The horses of the Sirdar's troopers are in miserable condition.

Náóróz Khan bears a very bad character, and is reported to be extremely treacherous, a trait unusual in a Balúch. He is now virtually ruler of Khárán, old Azád Khán being pretty well in his dotage. Náóróz Khán has quarrelled with his two brothers: Amir Khan, the elder, is now with the Khán of Kalát, while the younger, Azún Khán, has gone to his father-in-law Húsén Khán in the Garmsel. It is supposed one or both of these will endeavour to oust Náóróz Khán as soon as the old man is dead, and the latter is preparing for such a contingency, but it is doubtful whether the two younger brothers are not themselves at enmity.

The actual number of Náóshírwánís is very small, not more than 200 or 250. Fourteen men are land owners of more or less consequence. The remainder are mostly in Azád Khán's service. The total disposable force of Khárán is about 2,000 men. The greater number of these can be mounted on camels, consequently their movements are extremely rapid.

Friday, 30th December. KODAK (*Siriáb*). 19 miles. Leaving camp we took a shorter line and joined main track at the small mound near the fields; thus saving ½ a mile.

At 7 miles from Sorchíl (10½ from Bijar's well in Kodak), the road from Kalat by Sohráb, Mat, and Gidar, joins in.

* Probably obtained from the field of Maiwand. There is little doubt that a detachment from Khárán joined Ayúb Khán.

The Kalgali Pass of Cook and Malcolm Green is evidently the long narrow darah running up northwards from the upper (south) end of Besemar, between the high hills on the east side the valley. The guide knew the road went that way, but had never been along it.

He pointed out however the position of Zaiak, which is apparently rather off the direct line, under the hills on the right hand (east) side.

For this halting place, and the road to Sohráb, see reports by Major Malcolm Green and Dr. Cook (1860).

The open watershed at the north-east end of Besemar looks like a natural road way. By here must be the rough track mentioned by Cook as leading from Mát, and occasionally used by travellers to Khárán.

Shortly after passing the junction of the Gidar road, a path branches in the opposite direction, *i. e.* southwards, and is practically a continuation of the former.

It leads to Shíreza, which is as far from Sorchíl camp as Gwanak (about 25 miles) and therefore about 23 miles from Zaiak.

Here is a small village, fort, and cultivation. The place is in Azád Khan's territory, and the people are Rakhsháuí Balúch. Water from a small stream. The road is said to be practicable for camels.

The next stage, into the Rághaí valley, is as far as from Hokar to Sorchíl, (12 miles). Road fair.

Thence to Panjgúr is 4 stages of 16 to 18 miles each. Road practicable for camels, but water very scarce.*

Camped by the pools at the lower end of Kodak. It is the place called Kodak by Major M. Green, but the proper name of the spot is Siriáb, as the water here first appears in the nala.

The path diverges from that previously followed at the watershed, and is good and open all the way.

Water at Siriáb is abundant from pools in the bed of the nala, which is pretty thickly studded with large tamarisk. Wood and camel grazing abundant. Some natural grass; and after the harvest, bhoosa or kirbi would be procurable in small quantity. The cultivation is entirely khúshkáwa, and therefore barley is not to be expected.

Between the river bed and the hills to west are extensive gravelly flats, on which a very large force might encamp. The strip of low ground by the water is soft and sandy.

It appears that a generation or so ago,—within the memory of my informant, a man of about 60,—there were no less than 10 karazes in Kodak, and the spot was one of unusual fertility in this region. In the strife, however, between the Sájadís and the Súmalárís, these have either been allowed to become choked, or have been wilfully filled in by one or other party to prevent their rivals from making use of them, so that there is now no irrigated land in Kodak. Formerly Kodak and Korás were held by the Sájdis, but many years ago they were expelled from these lands by Seistan Balúchís. The latter were in turn ousted by the Súmalárís, as the natural expansion of the latter forced them to find outlets to the southward. The Sájadis, however, as original owners, still maintained their right to the lands, and are just strong enough to keep the Súmalárís from opening the karezes, without being able to regain possession for themselves.

---

* This is what we were told at the time; afterwards, when at Panjgúr, information collected from the best available sources made Shíreza 11 to 12 stages from Panjgúr. See Route XIV.

Probably both parties would not be sorry to come to a compromise, and if there was a tolerably strong government at Kalát peace would soon be restored.

The Súmaláris of Kodak and Korás give a contingent to Isúf Khan Mamasání (Mahomed Hasani) of Jibrí, who is the great man in these parts.

The Sájadis, as before mentioned, are allied to the Bizanjaos.

The Súmalári Sirdar (Lála or Lal Khán.) lives at Mat. The ancient home of the tribe was Sharó l, where (and in Shorawak) they are still pretty numerous Hereabouts, and everywhere west of Nál, the people move with their flocks in winter to Kolwah, and other warm districts of Mekran.

Of the Bizanjaos, some go to Sind, and some southward as far as Bela.

Saturday, 31st December.—Halted. Post came in this morning, having been as far as Pir Súltán on the Khárán road. There is a footpath (said to be impracticable for horses) straight from Nál to the lower end of Besemar—so the Kosid missed us.

Surveying and writing letters.

Sunday, 1st January 1882.—JAORI. 19 miles. Follow the river for some distance. It is good going, and the tamarisk trees are not thick enough to impede the march of troops. Low hills close in on the water course till about 2½ miles, when they cease.

The road now quits the nala and takes the left bank, crossing a stony plain which is the begining of Korás, a valley some 3 miles wide, now seen stretching away to the southward.

The Gúndáb road takes to the opposite bank, and also passing over a strip of stony plain, crosses a very low neck connecting a short detached ridge with the range on the right (west).

This is passed at 6 miles, and from thence to Gúndáb is about 6½ miles. Good road, keeping pretty close to the low ranges which here bound the valley on the west.

The position of Gúndab is easily recognized by an isolated low black hill, or rather rock, round which the river bed winds.

Water is tolerably abundant from a pool. Wood and camel grazing ditto.

Here the Dhúléri Nala coming from behind Múkh, joins the Kodak Nala (Kodak naju). There is a road up Dhúléri to Besemar, and it is considered the shortest way from Korás, but there is no water before reaching Sorchíl, a distance of over 30 miles.

What is of more importance, is the fact that there is a road westward to Panjgúr (No. IX.), and another by Shireza to Khurin (No. VII).

The people located at Gúndáb are Mahomad Hasánís, whose local chief is Yár Mahómad.

The Jaori road, going along on the left (east) side of the water course, touches it again at 6 miles opposite the detached hill inside of which the Gúndab road passes.

It continues nearly due south over the plain, which is of fine gravel, very bare, but flat and easy to travel over.

A 12 miles one is abreast of the Gúndáb rock, distant about 1½ miles.

On that side, the valley is seen to be bounded by some five or six rocky ridges, much lower than the hills to north and south, between which they form the connecting link. Beyond the ridges is a plain of some size, also called Korás.

On the east, the hills shutting in the valley, and separating it from Greshak, are quite low.

At 13 miles, cross the road from Greshak (i. e. from Nál and Wad) to Gúndáb and so to Sákán Kalát or Shíreza.

At 16 miles, pass, on the right hand side of the road, khushkawa cultivation called Madárgán. There is water in the low hills to left, but it is some distance off. People here are, I believe, Sájadís.

Thence, bending left, enter low hills, outliers of the broken chain to east. Although there are elevations of various height all round, the road is tolerably open and flat.

At 19 miles cross a broad water course, apparently the main drainage channel of Greshak. Banks easy. There is no water here, but in the next nala, a few hundred yards further on, are small pools, and the gravelly plateau between the two makes a very tolerable camping ground, sufficient to accommodate several battalions. To the east, is a short, but high and precipitous, ridge, the end of which is turned towards the spectator; beyond this again are lofty hills forming the main range. To the west are lower hills, on the further side of which, and about a mile distant, is the plain. To the south, beyond the nala, are more hills through which the road is continued.

Water rather scanty. Firewood tolerably abundant. No camel grazing in the immediate neighbourhood. No permanent habitations, here or anywhere near. The spot is a mere halting place, and one not much used.

Troops had better halt at Gúndáb, (12½) miles from Kodak Siriáb), and march thence to Jibrí, 15 miles. The road leads along the valley and is perfectly open and easy all the way. (See Route No. VIII).

A road leads from the Jáórí camping ground into Greshak through a gorge. Major M. Green says the "pass is reported rough." This is not the main road from Nál to Gwarjak; the latter goes straight to Jibrí.

Slight rain last night.

Monday, 22nd January.—JIBRI. 9 miles. Cross the nala in which is the water supply and ascend it for a few yards; then turn to right (S.) through the hills*. The path soon leads into a darah, as the main and outer ranges diverge. The darah gradually widens until about 4 miles from Jibrí when the inferior ranges on the right (W.) cease, and a wide stony plain is entered forming a part of the general valley.

Over this the road leads straight to Jibrí, the palm trees of which are visible at a considerable distance. It is good all the way.

The main route from Nál to Gwarjak joins in here, having passed the hills by the "Borída" defile. See reports of Major M. Green and Dr. Cook (1860).

At Jibrí is a large square tower on a low mound. It is described by Dr. Cook, and belongs to Sirdar Isúf Khan Mahomad Hasaní, a powerful chief. He lives without, as the death of several of his children in the fort, has caused that place to be shunned as a residence. It is, however, kept in tolerable repair, and is quite capable of making a good defence in local warfare.

The Sirdar himself and his people live in ghidans or *jumpris*. The frame work is of tamarisk, the walls and thatch of the inevitable *pish* (palmetto). They are not plastered with mud, and are decidedly inferior to the kirris of Shorá-

* See Reports by Major M. Green and Dr. Cook. I went back to survey, and thence straight down the valley.

wak to which they bear some resemblance. Here, however, as all over the Balúchistán highland, the people infinitely prefer their ghidans, or tabernacles, to any house, declaring the former to be warmer in winter and cooler in summer.

There are a good many date trees at Jibrí, clustering pretty thickly round the tower, and scattered away to the south for a mile or more. At the western base of the mound is a plantation of young fruit trees (pomgranates.) Beyond this, stretching up and down the valley for perhaps a mile each way, is cultivation, the *inam* land of the Sirdar.

It is watered by two small karez streams and rice is grown. There is also a little lucerne near the village. On the eastern side is a bare stony plain up to the base of the high hills.

At the present time there are about 60 huts in the neighbourhood of the fort.

There appears to be plenty of ground for encampment. Water is abundant, also camel grazing. Firewood tolerably plentiful. Grass from the hills. Bhoosa would be procurable in small quantities after the harvest, and some trifling amount of wheat and rice. Supplies, however, could be collected here by previous arrangement.

Isúf Khán is one of the most important Sirdars in Jhálawán. The nominal muster of Mahomed Hasanis is 18,000, but the tribe is very widely dispersed, and many may be found as far away as Sharód and Shorawak. With Lál Khán Súmalári's contingent, Isúf Khán might muster 5,000 men ; however he is very much thought of, and his "raj" said to extend over the whole country. Personally, the chief is a rather fine looking, quiet man, of about 50. He informed me that the Mahomed Hasanis came originally from Kirmán and Shiráz, and that his family had been settled at Jibrí for seven generations. "Formerly," " he added, the Ahmadzais* showed us great attention, and my forefathers had " large estates. Now however the Khán has seized everything, and though my " raj " may be great, my land does not extend to more than a rifle shot from my " tower."

Isúf Khan has never been in rebellion against the Khán of Kalát.

Jibrí is not considered as forming part of Mashkai, though it is one and the same valley. The former is Isúf Kháns inam, but the latter is all crown land.

Opposite Jibrí is a rather conspicuous hill, jutting out into the valley : it is called Shekh. The big hill on the east side is Mahmai.

Tuesday 3rd January.—RIND. (1,325 feet.) 7½ miles. South west down the valley. At about a mile from the fort, is a small pond, the tail of one of the karezes. Here is boundary between Mashkai and Jibrí. Beyond, is a grove of date palms, and some cultivation. Thence the road keeps along the western base of an isolated ridge, and when this ceases, enters on a stony tract formed by the detritus brought down the numerous water courses of the eastern hills. It is thickly grown with pish, which here covers an area of several square miles. The pish is mixed with tamarisk.

The road is good, over slaty gravel. Some date groves in front show the existence of water. At about 6½ miles cross a small irrigation-channel. This is from a karez called Nókjo (see Major M. Green's report). On the right is cultivation. A little further on, a few hundred yards to left of the road, is a mound, with the remains of a fort. It belongs to Yar Mahomed Kéhar, whose toman of pish huts was visible at no great distance to the south east. To north

* *Ahmadzais.* The ruling family at Kalát.

east was another toman of Kéhars under Sháfí Mahomed. These tomans are nearly always in the same places. In very severe weather only, do they move off, and take shelter under the eastern range.

At 7½ miles Rind; a karez, cultivation and date trees, resembling Nókjo. Wood and water abundant; also camel grazing; grass procurable.

Ground for encampment would no doubt be found without difficulty on the cultivable land. The site would depend on the crops.

The valley has now reached its widest, and is about 10 miles across, but the cultivable land seems to be barely a mile in width.

Wednesday, 4th January.—GAJAR. (4,120 feet.) 10 miles. South-west towards a conspicuous isolated hill. Good road over the same slaty gravel. Tamarisk, písh, and other shrubs, with a few small trees, are pretty thickly scattered over the country.

At 4 miles the hill is reached, and the track runs parallel to its base. As soon as it is passed the road divides; that leading to Gajar, bends half right, while the other leads straight on to Parwar and Gwarjak.*

The Gajar road soon gets among the broken alluvial ground in the neighbourhood of the river bed.

The cultivation becomes almost continuous and groups of huts are met with.

At about 6½ miles a channel of the river bed is crossed; banks low and easy.

The road continues to wind through very broken ground, among numerous half silted up channels. Tamarisk and other bushes grow thickly on all sides.

At 9½ miles reach, and cross, the main channel of the river bed. It is broad and shallow, the width being about 150 yards. A small perennial stream runs in it. Here begin the date groves of Gajar, both banks of the river being thickly planted with these trees for a considerable distance.

On the right bank is a hamlet called Mandi Mach (*mach*—a date tree). Thence through the date trees for half a mile to Gajar, which is a poor looking village of some 30 or 40 permanent huts near the base of an artificial hillock crowned by a ruined fort.

The people here are Kéhars; there are altogether about 100 families scattered up and down the banks of the river. These Kéhars call themselves Baluch, but are I believe Jats. They are a poor harmless race, and are exclusively cultivators, farming the lands of Mashkai which belong to the Khán. By religion they are Dáhís (or Zikars), as are also the Sájdí Bráhúís. Cook gives an account of their tenets and morality which I suspect has been derived from Mussulman accounts, and to be much exaggerated. Their language is Mekrání Balúch.

All Mashkai is Mahomed Hasani country, under Isúf Khán of Jibrí, and the pastoral people are mostly of that tribe.

The fort of Gajar was built by Nasír Khán 1st of Kalát. It is now entirely dismantled, but the stout rubble walls, 6 to 8 feet high in most places, and the steep sides of the mound, also of rubble, still make it a very defensible redoubt in native warfare. The palm trees, however, grow close up to the base of the mound on the east side.

---

* This hill, and the next detached one, which is opposite Gajar, are called Láki. The one above mentioned is that which Dr. Cook visited in search of the remains of an ancient city.

There are no banias at Gajar, and no watermills. Corn is ground by hand. Barley was sold at 14 seers for the rupee, wheat at 10½ seers. The cost of grinding is considerable. In summer, prices would no doubt be much lower. Sufficient grain is grown in the country to feed a considerable force passing through, but previous notice would have to be given.

The *dáman* of the western range comes right down to the village. There is any amount of room for encampment, but the ground is stony.

Wood, water, and camel grazing abundant. Grass of the sort called *kándár* is abundant. The water of the river is slightly saline.

Thursday, 5th January.—Halted. Post in this morning. Writing letters, &c. Obliged to change camels here, and there is some difficulty in getting them.

Wednesday, 6th January.—Halted. Surveying.

The river channel is 100 to 200 yards broad. Beds of high reeds and flags* fringe the low shelving banks. The running stream only begins about 1½ or 2 miles above Gajar. Higher up there are occasional pools.

It is called the *Dhuléri*. The Chákar is the Kodak nála. The water is drawn off for irrigation, but only a very narrow strip so benefits. However, there is a good deal of fine khushkawa land, carefully banked, and the water of the hill torrents is mostly utilized. The date groves are almost continuous, on both sides, to Parwar about 6 miles below. Their produce is abundant, but of inferior quality.

Pomegranates are also grown pretty extensively. In flood time the Dhuléri completely fills its bed, overflowing the low cultivable land, and sometimes coming right up to the base of the mound on which the old fort is built.†

The Naib of the district is Abdul Karím, Mírwári Sirdar, of Kólwah. He lives at Bédí, close to Awarán in Kólwah. The Jánishín (one Bákshi a Khánazád) has a house here, and one at Parwar.

On the opposite side of the river, about a mile distant, is a Kambaráni hamlet connected with a village of the same tribe lower down. It has about 10 huts.

Two miles from Gajar fort is a hamlet of about 20 huts of Kéhars. It is situated at the base of a low range of hills, which extends from about 1½ miles above Gajar to Parwar, or about seven miles altogether. They run parallel, and close to, the river bed the whole way, and the hill drainage comes *through* them by three or four rather narrow gaps. These hills have rounded summits and easy slopes, and are traversable in every direction by horsemen.

The Kambaráni village (called *Bánsar*) is about 4 miles below Gajar on the same side (right bank). It contains about 30 huts,‡ and a conspicuous fort, with a tower or high building in it. Perched as usual on a hillock, it stands out against the palm trees as approached from the east, and is quite a feature in the landscape.

Every village, or cluster of villages, has one of these forts, intended as a place of refuge for the people in case of attack, but otherwise left empty

---

* Pig are found in these.

† The floods occur in July or August. The Dhuléri goes by Manguli to Awarán and is the head of the Hingol River.

‡ A majority of the huts are made of reeds and pish; but some are of rubble, mortared or plastered with mud. The wood of the date palm is used in building.

and uninhabited. They are built of rubble, plastered with mud, and no doubt serve well the purpose for which they are constructed. The mud is very light coloured, and at a distance buildings plastered with it have the appearance of being white-washed.

The chief of the Kambaránís is Mahomed Fazl,* and their lands are *inam*.

A short distance below Kambaráni, and opposite to the termination of the low hills on the left bank, is a Mírwárí village known as Mían Kalát.

Parwar is also at the end of the low range, but on the east side, close to their base, and its fort is on a knoll, one of the last spurs of the hills.

Parwar consists of two villages, known as Jagasur and Buturú. They are mostly inhabited by Mírwárís, and with the third village mentioned above (Mian Kalát), and scattered groups, there are upwards of 300 huts of that tribe. The local chief is Pir Mahomed, son of the late Shabák. Ghúlam Mahomed is an important man and head of a section.

There is a little *inam* land, but most of it is held by the Mírwárís from the Khán.

From Nókjo downwards, the valley may be considered as really well wooded. Except the date palms, however, there are no trees of any size; but small mimosas, tamarisks, &c., are in thousands, and dot the stony *dáman* nearly up to the base of the rocky hills; while the písh covers many hundred acres.

Thursday, 7th January.—Halted. Despatched post. Surveying.

Wheat and barley ripen here in April. The barley about a fortnight earlier than the wheat. Second crops are rice and jowárí. These are reaped three, or three and a half, months after the first crops. About the same time the date harvest comes on.

It is at this season that heavy rain and thunderstorms are expected. The winter rains are comparatively light, and probably uncertain. Snow falls in the valley occasionally, but does not lie.

The maximum of the thermometer in the shade, since we have been here, has been about 78°, and the minimum about 36°. In summer the heat is great, but of course there are no hot winds.

The people deny the unhealthiness ascribed to the place by Cook. It is acknowledged however, that strangers always fall ill in summer; but this may be ascribed in great part to their over-eating themselves with fresh dates, of which both Brahúís and Balúch are inordinately fond.

At Gajar are 30 blacksmiths, but they are not working now as they have no iron.

One leather worker here, and one at Parwar.

One bania is resident at Parwar, but at harvest time many visit the valley from Kalát and elsewhere.

The hill in the western range (for which, as usual, there is no general name) exactly abreast of Gajar, is called Kúkí. There is a water in a big ravine, known as Kúkí spring.

To north of the hill is a foot-path, called Jání, across the range. It is practicable, but difficult, for horses. The descent is into a narrow *darah*, on the further side of which is another range which cannot be seen over from the crest of this(?) Beyond that again is *Rághái*, a large valley, but a man on foot cannot get there in one day. Beyond Rághái is *Rashkán*, which is bounded on the further side by a high range of the same manner.

---

* He lives at Kalát.

Rághái and Rashkán belong to Azád Khán. Rashkán or Rakshán is divided from Gitchk by a range which is Azád Khán's boundary.

The Gandáp road goes down Rághái and into the Gitchk valley. The direct road from Kalát by Shiréza also leads, by Kapar, into Rághái and in Gitchk they both meet the road from Gwarjak to Panjgúr.*

Friday, 8th January.—HALTED. Camels at last turned up this evening, Isúf Khan's sowars having been scouring the country for 4 days to get them. It is absolutely necessary to carry supplies for the whole distance between this and Panjgúr—11 camel stages.

Although I have had time to take a tolerably good look at all the ground in the immediate vicinity of Gajar, I can find no spot which would make a really decent camping ground. The best spot is probably the stony flat, south west of the fort; but this is broken by small nálas. The low ground near the river is pretty nearly always under crops of some sort. Troops arriving just after either of the harvests, say the latter end of April or August, would be able to utilize this land, but not otherwise. All the uncultivated ground is either very stony and jungly, or broken, or all three.

Cloudy to day, and slight rain before sunset.

The clouds came up with a light south west wind, as on the 1st. The northerly winds drive away the rain.

Saturday, 9th January.—GWARJAK. 10½ miles. (2,964 feet.) Slight rain last night, but the morning was fine, though a southerly wind and clouds coming up betokened wet before long.

Followed the right bank of the river bed.

The road leads along the edge of the date grove and cultivation. On the right is the stony *dáman* stretching up to the base of the hills about 3½ miles distant.

Soon after passing the last date trees cross rising ground. A low elevation is between the road and the river. Beyond this is cultivation, across which the track leads when irrigation operations are not going on. Otherwise it must be avoided by a detour over rather stony and broken ground.

As far as this the country is open from the river up to the base of the eastern range; but from 4 miles below Gajar to beyond Gwarjak there is a mass of inferior hills, sinking lower and lower from the main range, and filling up the whole of the intervening space. In the neighbourhood of the river they are of no height and can be traversed by cavalry.

At about 6 miles pass the village of Bánsar, which, with its date groves and cultivation, lies between these low hills and the river.

It has been before described. The fort is rather dilapidated, but not so much so as most, and lies a few hundred yards to left of the road.

Thence pass over a very low spur to Míiu Kalát, which is reached at 7 miles. It is similarly situated to Bánsar. The fort is quite ruinous.

The road here approaches close to the river for a short distance. It then passes over stony, and slightly rough, ground. On the opposite side of the river is Parwar, almost hidden behind the low hills on that side. Below Parwar, but rather back from the river, is a hamlet and date groves called Konéró. It contains about 15 huts of Mírwárís. On the right bank the low hills trend back for some distance.

* We saw Rághái, Gitchk, and Rashkán in our way to Panjgúr. See Diary further on, and also Map.

On the left of the road is cultivation. This ceases at about 8½ miles, and its termination marks the limit of the Khan's territory, and the commencement of the little district of Gwarjak which belongs to Azád Khán.

On the other side the river, but some little distance below (about due south), two date trees growing together are the boundary land mark.

The river is now bordered, first on the right, and afterwards, as it winds, on the left, by large reed beds.

At 9 miles is the commencement of a line of conglomerate bluffs, between which and the river the road passes for half a mile, crossing two water-courses.

At 9½ miles cross the river bed diagonally. It here makes a rather sharp bend to the westward. Gwarjak is situated in this bend; the fields and date groves on the left bank, the village and fort on the right, the former under the conglomerate hills, the latter perched on a semi-isolated bluff, scarped on all sides. It is about 120 feet above the river bed, and of the construction usual in this country, perhaps rather larger and better, but by no means in perfect repair. That is to say the outer wall is dilapidated and looks low, but the keep seems in good order. It has a double tier of loop holes. There is no path to the fort. People are drawn up and let down by ropes. Green says there is a well in the fort.

Násír Khán IInd tried to take it and failed; but as it is actually lower than other bluffs above, and small hills below, it is probable that even mountain guns would be able to render it untenable.

Azád Khan has a Kotwal in charge of the fort, by name Basham, and with him are a few *ghulâms*, but no regular garrison.

The village consists of about 30 huts of Naoshírwání Balúch, the rais or chief man among whom is Gámguzár. No bannias now reside at Gwarjak, though there were some a year or two back. There is a family of goldsmiths here, who are also blacksmiths.

The best camping ground appears to be half a mile south, on the left bank, but, as at Gajar, there is no very good place. There is some cultivated ground on the right bank, which would do, if clear of crops.*

It began to rain about 2 o'clock and there were several smart showers during the afternoon. It also rained in the night.

The best way from Gajar to Gwarjak is to take at once to the river bed, and follow it to Mián Kalat whence the road is the same as that given above. Artillery would keep to the river bed all the way, and it is but little longer. Both roads are good for laden camels.

Wood, water, camel grazing and forage, are abundant. No supplies, except small quantities of barley and wheat.

Sunday, 10th January.—TANK. (3764 feet). 9½ miles.

Follow the river bed for about a mile and a half, when the road ascends gravelly plateaux on the right bank. Over these it passes for 4½ miles in a south-south-westerly direction, while the river bed keeps away to the south. The track ascends and descends over the undulations of the plateaux, which are broken, and traversed by water-courses from the hills. The road however, is good.

Soon after quitting the river an immense number of *gaur-bastas* are passed. In some places the walls are 5 and 6 feet high, and all those which are visible from the road appear to have been, as usual, terraces, or bunds, to retain

---
* Major M. Green appears to have camped here. 15th March 1860.

rain water for agricultural purposes. If so, the black, sterile, and rugged plain must then have been well cultivated. It is, however, difficult to imagine that such could ever have been the case.

This appears to be the ruined city mentioned by Cook.

At 6 miles descend from the plateaux into the valley, or hollow, of the Tank steam, which issues from a defile about a mile to the west.

Tank means *tangi*, and the stream is so called from the defiles through which it runs. Here its bed is quite as large as that of the Dhuléri. The flow of water is greater, and its valley is thickly wooded with tamarisk, and also with trees of larger growth. Running on, about south-east, it passes through low hills and joins the Dhuléri at 3 miles from where it leaves the hills.*

Beyond the point now reached the country is quite new and unexplored.

The road turns up the Tank, through tamarisk jungle. The stream is crossed at 1½ miles, and at 7½ one is fairly within the defile.

The hills on either side are of considerable height, that to right is called Bambakán and the other Doráskí.† These are part of the range bounding Mashkai, &c., on the west, but are of sufficient size to be noticeable as far off as Jibrí, over 30 miles in a straight line. The defile winds between spurs of the above. Its average width is about 50 to 60 yards, and the heights in immediate proximity are comparatively inconsiderable, though often steep and craggy.

The stream is crossed frequently, but is quite shallow, with gravelly bottom. Road an easy camel track.

Camped at 9½ miles on a *bend* or plateau on the left bank.

Wood and water abundant. Camel grazing rather scanty. Grass from the hills abundant. The water is better than that of the Dhuléri. General direction of this march S. S. W.

Monday, 11*th January*.—KUCHKÁN. (4,057 feet). 8½ miles. Followed the river bed. The pass is of the same general character. At first the hills are higher, afterwards, as the main range is passed, they are of less elevation.

Average breadth of the pass about 50 yards.

The running stream is rather increased than diminished in volume.

In the 3rd and 4th miles (5th and 6th from camping ground at entrance of pass) the fords are comparatively deep, being 2 feet in places, but the crossings are all easy, except one at about 3 miles, where there are large stones under water on the landing side.

Immediately after this, a small but rather high *bend* (plateau) is crossed. Ascent and descent steep, but not difficult.

Generally the path keeps to the river bed, only leaving it occasionally for a few hundred yards to make a short cut over good ground.

Here and there rough slaty rocks are passed over, but for the most part the track is good.

However, the accumulative difficulties of water and rocks, though insignificant in themselves, make this march somewhat trying to laden animals, quite as much so to mules as to camels.

At 7 miles (9 from camp at mouth of pass) is the halting place called Gwánk Músht (a meaningless name from *gwánk*, a shout : *musht*, a fist or

---

* The junction is called *Tank-na-bah*, i.e., " mouth of the Tank." It was subsequently visited.
† Súrgarh (?).

handful). Here is stony ground on the right bank sufficient for two battalions to encamp, but it is rough and inconvenient.

There is, however, an abundance of camel grazing in the shape of tamarisk, for which reason it is one of the regular camel stages.

Went on a mile and a half to Kúchkán, where there is also good camel grazing.

After Gwánk Musht, numerous willow trees grow along the sides of the pass, and high grass begins to fringe the edge of the stream in places.

Wood and water abundant also hill grass of good quality, called *gurkáo*.

There is plenty of room in this halting place, but the ground is uneven, stony, and grown with tamarisk. A flat below grown with willow trees, and also part of Kúchkán, would be probably more convenient.*

The mass of hills traversed since entering the defile consists, as usual, of parallel ranges of greater or less height, running north-north-east and south-south-west. Formation chiefly clay slate, at least such I should call it, and Dr. Cook gives it the same name, but it is identical with the eocene shales of the Kwájha Amrán and Sarlat ranges, of which these hills are in some sort a continuation.

Trap intrusions are however very frequent. The higher hills are often banded by dark trappoid rocks, and the lower ranges entirely composed of the same. The shale beds also are constantly seen to be crushed and distorted, and converted into metamorphic rock.

The hills extend far, both to north and south; in the latter direction they are said to divide Kólwah from Kéj.† On the left bank of the stream, i.e., to north, the country belongs to Khárán; on the other side to the Gitchkís; but the whole is a common (summer) grazing ground for Mahomed Hasanis, Sájdís, Gitchkís, &c. At Kúchkán were some huts of Kóhars, who possess a herd of buffaloes which are kept for making ghi. These Kóhars have to pay a tenth of the increase of their cattle to Azád Khán. The latter also takes *sung*, or toll, from all who pass this way.

The general direction of this march is west.

As might be expected, signs of high floods in the defile are not infrequent. Drift wood and dead trees show that the river bed is sometimes filled to a height of 8 feet. The people say that a rise of 20 feet has been known. This is probably an exaggeration, but 4 feet rise would completely fill the channel, and render the pass altogether impracticable. It must be borne in mind that the stream appears to have a very large catchment basin.

The season for floods is July and August.

Cold north-east wind to-day has entirely blown away the rain.

Tuesday, 12th January.—PASHT KOH CAMP. (4,194 feet.) 9 miles. Meant to have gone on further, as also yesterday, but the camel men are troublesome, their beasts being in bad condition. As it was, the difficulty of surveying gave me a very fair day's work.

From Kúchkán the hills begin to be decidedly lower, and the country shows signs of opening out. The river bed increases in width to 100 yards or more. In fact the road is now hardly through a defile.

At about 5 miles is a sort of valley filled only by low ridges and hillocks.

---

* I think "kuchkán" means willows.

† This is not the case. Kólwah and Kéj are continuous, *i.e.*, divided only by a watershed. See diary further on.

Here, on the left bank, is some cultivation and about 20 huts of Sájdís. The place is called Pasht Kóh i.e. "beyond the hills," rather a misnomer.

About a mile and a half beyond this enter another belt of hills of no great elevation but of considerable thickness. The defile by which they are traversed is about 60 to 80 yards wide, but the heights on either hand (mostly clay slate) are easily accessible.

The kaŭla halting place known as Pasht Kóh is within these hills, and it therefore belies its name. It is (as usual) on a bent, or flat, and is on the right bank of the water-course. There is room for a battalion to encamp, but the ground is sandy and stony, commanded by hills on all sides, and generally unsuitable. Wood, water, camel grazing, and hill grass (gúrkáo) abundant.

At Pasht Kóh hamlet is certainly the best place for troops to halt, and it might be reached in one march of about 16 miles from the entrance of the defile. It would, however, be rather a trying stage to baggage animals.

The road from Kúchkán is good all the way. General direction north-north-west.

To-day was fine and warm.

Wednesday, 13*th January*.—SAKAN KALAT. Elevation, 4345 feet. 380 feet higher than Gwarjak. 10¼ miles.

The road winds through the hills for more than 2 miles, after which they become low and broken. Here, immediately after passing through the higher ridges, is the junction of the Rághai nala with the Gitchkí stream. When united they form the Tank. The former comes from the north; the latter from the west, and is much the larger. The running water comes down the Gitchkí while the Rághai is dry or nearly so.

At the junction ascend left bank of the Gitchkí, and passing through thick tamarisk jungle for 100 yards, cross a small tract of uneven country surrounded by low hills. This cuts off a bend of the stream.

At 3½ miles pass irrigated fields and a few huts of Kétchí Sájdís on the left bank of the Gitchkí. The place is called Darkaví.

Beyond this the river bed is entered and followed for a short distance through the hills. It is then finally quitted, and the path ascends a branch nala to the right (north-west) through broken ground and low elevations.

At about 5 miles is a long bank from which issue numerous saline springs. The ground is covered with coarse grass, and soft from the quantity of water. This place is called Sand.

Just above the bank is a very low ridge, or line of hillocks, and a few hundred yards further is another. On gaining the crest of the latter a wide plain suddenly appears, extending from one's feet to a considerable range in front, about 8 miles distant, and to right and left (north-east and south-west) for a great distance.

As usual this plain has no one name. To the north is Rághai and beyond that is Kapar, which is about the watershed. These places belong to Khárán. Rághai does not come down quite so low as the road. The boundary is the Ahór nala which issues from the opposite hills nearly due north of Sand.

There is no cultivation in Rághai nor are there any permanent inhabitants. It is a grazing ground for Mahomed Hasánís, Sájdís, Bakshánís, &c.

Next to Rághai and immediately in front is Kásbán A'p which belongs to Sájdís. This is a small tract.

South of Káshán A'p is Gitchk.*

Beyond the hills is Rashkán, part of Khárán territory. The range is known generally as Rashkán-na-lat.

From the ridge the descent to the plain is only a few feet. At first the path lies across rough ground thickly grown with grass in high tussocks. This is evidently pretty often flooded. Beyond are shallow dry water-courses in which are a few water-holes. Here is Káshán-áp halting place. Afterwards an expanse of fine gravel and sand is entered. This, often rising into low undulations, forms the greater part of the plain. It is pretty thickly sprinkled with babúl trees, tamarisk, and other shrubs.

At about 2 miles are low hillocks, on the left. There are others further off on the right. At $2\frac{1}{2}$ miles strike the well marked track which comes down through Rághai from Gandáp and Shíréza. This is followed for a short distance, and then, as Sákán Kalat becomes visible, a straight line is taken to that place.

Sákán Kalát is small rude fort placed as usual on a mound. It is of irregular rectangular form, the longest interior diameter being about 32 yards. Walls of rubble 8 to 10 feet high and 1 foot to 18 inches thick. They are in tolerable preservation, but the huts built, according to custom, against the walls inside are ruinous. A very small doorway on the south can only be entered by stooping. There is a well in the interior of the fort. It is about 50 feet deep, and there are two or three feet of rubbish at the bottom. If this was cleared away there would be plenty of water.

On the west side of the mound is a patch of cultivation watered by two small karezes,† and scattered about are some 20 húts of Mahomed Hasánís, who are "bazgars" of the Sájdís or Sáká to whom the land belongs.

Camping ground good; it lies west and south-west of the fort, between cultivation and low rising ground. Wood and water abundant, also barshón grass. Camel grazing rather scanty.

Fine clear day. This place, as might be expected from its high and open situation, is perceptibly colder than Mashkai or the Tank defiles. We have now entered Mekrán.

Thursday 14*th January*.—Halted. Surveying. Warmer to-day and slightly cloudy.

About 4 miles south-west are 20 families of Sásúlís. The people hereabouts do not migrate, there being grazing for their sheep all the year round. A few Rakshánís, however, go down to the plain of Khárán.

There is no other cultivation than that at Sákán Kálat in the whole valley. In fact there is surprisingly little ground capable of cultivation, and what there is, is poor thin soil.

Friday, 15*th January.*—SARAP (Sir-i-áb). Elevation, 4321 feet. 13 miles. Southwards from Sákán Kalat, over the gravelly plain studded with babúl, &c., for about 3 miles, when the main road is struck, and followed in a south westerly direction. It leads along the south-east side of the Gitchkí valley. On the left, but some little way off, are hills, at first almost imperceptible but rising higher as they recede. To the south they begin to run east and west instead of north east and south west. On the right, about 6 miles distant, is the Rashkán range. A good deal of the intermediate ground consists of low, bare, gravelly undulations.

---

* It is from this place the Gitchki clan derives its name.

† Formerly there were more, but the others have long since been choked.

After 6 miles the trees &c. cease, and from thence is an almost perfectly open plain of fine gravel and sand rising very gradually but steadily. The drainage from the hills appears to spread so much that the water-courses (running from right to left) are hardly perceptible.

At about 11 miles a line of jungle, crossing the front and coming round to the left, shows the course of the Gitchkí nala, last seen in the low hills before reaching Sand.

The main track is now quitted, as the water is below the road, i. e. to the left front, and a straight line taken to the halting place.

Camped on the nala, which was in several channels, amid broken, sandy, and rather thickly wooded ground. The water is in pools here and there; it is stagnant but sweet. There is apparently plenty of it;* and wood, camel grazing, and barshón grass are abundant. The best place for the encampment of troops would be beyond the watercourses.

Passed to-day some Mahomad-Hasiní shepherds, and a katila of about 25 Sumákárí camels laden with Panjgúr dates.

Excellent road all the way.

Saturday, 16th January.—SARGWAZ. Elevation, 4646 feet, 14½ miles.

Southwest over the same open, gravelly, and gently rising plain. The track is now about in the centre of the valley.

At 5 miles is a well, near, but not noticeable, from the road.

At 7 miles, about half a mile to left of the track, is a mound, crowned by the fragmentary remains of an old Gitchkí fort. On the south side is a well, evidently much used for watering flocks. We estimated the depth at about 50 feet. There appeared to be plenty of water.

At 10 miles, a third well close to the road on the right hand side. Estimated depth 60 or 70 feet. Water abundant and good.

At 12 miles, a solitary tree, about 300 yards to right of the road, is a land mark.

At 14 miles, Sargwaz.† Here is a well several hundred yards to left of the road. Beyond the well is a mound which serves to mark its position very exactly. The well is a large one, 100 feet deep, and contains several feet of good water. It does not appear to be much used. Any amount of ground for encampment in the open plain. Wood and camel grazing at some little distance to south east. Barshón grass abundant in the same direction.

Road excellent all the way.

Passed to-day a Bizanjáo kafila of 20 camels, 2 bullocks, and 14 donkeys, laden with Panjgúr dates and bound for Nál.

The watershed of Gitchkí is about 8 miles distant. It elevation must be nearly 5000 feet. Beyond, the country is called Gwárgŭ. It continues open like Gitchkí for an indefinite distance.

Sunday, 17th January.—MANCHAR. Elevation, 5004 feet. 11¾ miles.

West over the plain, ascending steadily, to foot of low black hills. Here, at 4½ miles, is a well called Darhanár (Darah Hanár—"pomgranate valley," or "hollow." There actually were some pomgranates at one time, but none now). This name is also applied to the surrounding tract, which contains some khúshkáwa

---

* The people say there is never any less. Running water does not begin in the Gichki for a good way down, "about opposite to Sákán Kalát."

† The name appears to mean "head of the valley" and is applied to the whole tract up to the watershed.

land, a subject of dispute between A'zád Khán and the Gitchkís.* The road skirts the hills for a short distance, and then crossing a dry watercourse (easy) continues, in the same direction as before, diagonally through low parallel ridges mostly composed of crumbling trap.

At about 6 miles cross a watershed.† Thence descend gradually widening water courses through low hills and clay slate plateaux. The fall is rapid, and the nalas are sunk deep below the level of the rough tract through which they run, and which is known as Ghar.

At about 7 miles pass some water in the nala bed. At 8 miles leave the water-course and pass to the right, over higher ground, to another. The drainage of all these goes south-west to Gwárgú. The nala now entered is followed round to north, and then again to west and south-west to the halting place.

Here are 2 or 3 small water holes, and there is really no place to encamp except the bed of the nala which is about 15 yards across. It is however very smooth and even. As for the water supply, each hole only appears to contain about as much as a wash hand basin; but the water runs below the surface and they do not become exhausted. Digging would ensure a tolerable amount. Wood and grass are scanty, and there is no camel grazing.

Troops would not halt here, except for some special reason, and would then be obliged to bivouac in the bed of the nala. The hills on either side are several hundred feet high but quite accessible.

Road good all the way. The nala beds are of fine slaty gravel or shingle and are easy travelling. The track is well marked.

The word Mánchar means a loop or bend.

Monday 18*th January*—ZAIAK. 4577 feet. 14 miles. Ascend the nala, which narrows and rises rather rapidly. Some very sharp turns would require cutting out for artillery. Road smooth; in one place there is a ledge about a foot high. There is surface water in several places above camp.

At 1½ miles the "kand" or crest of the pass. The last hundred yards is steep, increasing from 1 in 15 to 1 in 12.

From heights near the crest a good view can be obtained of the surrounding country. To the south-east and east Gitchk; to the south-west and west Gwárgú. Beyond these is a mass of parallel ranges of no great height separating them from Kólwah. To the north and north-east is Rashkán, a broad but broken valley, extending for a great distance. High ranges on the further side can be traced for at least 50 miles in a north easterly direction. Khárán bears a few degrees east of north; but the road lies up Rakshán and, leaving Shiréza on the right, passes through the hills. To the west is Panjgur, its plain being a continuation of Rashkán.

From here also the structure of the range, in a series of broken ridges running parallel to one another, is very noticeable. This is the normal formation of all the hills in this country. The mass of the range is clay slate, but trap, in a more or less disintegrated state, is everywhere intrusive, and so mixed as it were with the original beds that it is often difficult to tell what a hill is really made of. Dykes of trap crown almost every ridge.

Descent from the crest of the pass is by an easier gradient than the ascent; but the water course is very narrow, and somewhat rough from the fragments

---

* Kafilas sometimes halt here, but there is not much water.

† A road from Kolwah through the hills (south-south-west), and across the plain, joins in about this point. It is a good camel road and is used by kafilas.

of trap which have fallen into it. The camel track, however, is smooth and good. There is water in several places for the first mile.

At first the direction is to north-west, but at about 4 miles the water-course is quitted and a branch followed to the left (west) which leads to a Kotal (5075 feet). Ascent and descent easy, but nalas are narrow. From thence gain a second main ravine, which is also quitted shortly afterwards, and another watershed (5050 feet) passed over into a third ravine. This last Kotal is also quite easy, and the surrounding clay slate hills are low, and easily traverseable by infantry.

The ravine now entered is followed for several miles. It widens considerably and the hills sink into conglomerate undulations. A water hole is passed at about 8 miles. Either here or in the neighbourhood is the halting place called *Jáish.**

Unfortunately it was almost dark when we got to this point and we could only think of getting on as fast as possible.

At about 13½ miles turn abruptly to the left and proceed over low undulations to the bed of another water-course. Here is the halting place, at the foot of the hills, about a mile off the main road. The nala is broad, and lies between conglomerate plateaux, on which ground might be found for the encampment of troops, but they are broken by hollows and there is not much room in any one place.

The water runs under the left bank of the nala. It comes from a long way up, but sinks into the stones at the camping place. No doubt a good supply might be got near the road by digging. It is very slightly saline.

Wood and camel grazing moderate. Grass tolerably plentiful.

Tuesday 19th January.—Halted. Surveying.

Rashkán is a very large valley 12 to 16 miles in width and of great length. Its watershed is said to be 9 or 10 camel stages north-east of the centre of Panjgúr and not less than 100 miles distant. The valley is drained by a large water-course (Kaur) also called Rashkán. This is dry.

Rashkán appears to consist almost entirely of bare flats of dark gravel and small shingle sloping gently down to the water-course. In other words the dámán of the hills on either side actually abuts on the Rashkán Kaur, and there is no centre of alluvial soil as is commonly the case. The aspect of the valley is very barren and desolate.

As might be expected there is hardly any cultivation. At a place called Nágh, or Nágha Kalát, 6 or 7 stages from Panjgúr (see route No. XIV.†), there is a little irrigated land, and in one or two spots are patches of khushkáwa The country, however, is good for sheep.

The inhabitants of Rashkán are mostly Mahomed Hasánís, but beyond Nágh are "Nasrúí" Balúch.

Azád Khán's boundary, according to the Gitchkís of Panjgúr, is at Kénagí, a well about 50 miles from Isáí. I believe, however, he claims right up so Pír Umar, and even pretends to have a right to Panjgúr itself.

The road to Shíréza Kalát by Route XIV.† lies right up the Kaur. A

---

* Troops would probably halt here. Distance from Sargwaz 19½ miles. From Darbanár 15 miles. Jáish to Pír Umar 14 miles.

† I think the distances given in route XIV. are all exaggerated. Perhaps some stages have got in which do not belong to the route at all, as there are several tracks up the valley and my informants may have got confused, though I did my best to sift their statements. At all events the distances will not plot as they stand. Probably Kénagí well is only 30 to 35 miles from Isáí.

branch road to Wáshúk goes from about the centre of the valley over the Soráni Kand. (See routes XI. and XII.)

The three passes into Gitchk and Rághai have been already mentioned. They are the Gharái to north, Múrgáp from Sakán Kalát in the centre, and to south the Ghar road by which we came. South again of Ghar there is a pass known the Sháhmi Kand (afterwards explored), from Panjgúr into Gwárgú; it is practicable, but difficult, for laden camels.

Wednesday, 20th January.—PIR UMAR. 1273 feet. 8 miles. Down the watercourse for a short distance and then bear away to the left (west) over a broad gravelly plain gently sloping to the Kaur, which is some miles distant on the right.

The road is remarkably level and good, and the palm trees of Pír Umar are visible almost the entire distance.

A short way before reaching them the road enters a large but shallow hollow, passes along it, and again ascends the right bank,

Here is the Ziárat of Pír Umar with a few date trees and a patch of cultivation. There is also a mat hut village of fakírs. Amír Khan, younger brother of Mir Gájián, Gitchki Chief and Naib of Panjgúr, resides here on account of a family quarrel.

To west and north of Pír Umar is an extensive undulating plain of black gravel, affording ample room for encampment. Water abundant. Grass moderate. Camel grazing and wood rather scanty. Supplies procurable from Sir-i-Kaurán, Sordu, &c., 3 or 4 miles north-west.

Received here by the Naib and a large following.

Thursday, 21st January.—ISAI. 4122 feet. 10 miles. Road at first west-north-west. The hollow mentioned above comes round Pir Umar and is now crossed again. Descent and ascent very easy. It joins the Kaur about 2 miles below the road, and through the opening there is a glimpse of a long line of date groves in which are the villages of Sir-i-Kaurán and Wajhbúd.

South of the Kaur the centre of the valley is occupied by a gently undulating plateau of dark gravel, between which and the southern range is a space of lower lying country. All the villages of Panjgúr, imbedded in date trees, are along the Kaur, so that the fertile strip is a very narrow one. The road strikes this at Sordú (3½ miles), and here, where the gravel plateau slopes to the palm groves, is the residence of Mir Gájián, a large and comfortable castellated house. Adjacent is a small village of mat huts. The road, bending west, a few hundred yards short of Sordú, skirts the plateau. One village after another is passed, each hidden among its own date trees, the groves of which are almost continuous from Sir-i-Kauran to Isái. Khudabadán, on the opposite, or right, bank of the Kaur, is passed at about 7 miles.

Camped at Isái this side (i. e. east) of the fort and village. Water and supplies abundant, but camel grazing is scanty and so is grass.

The Sirdár and his cortége joined us at Sordú, and we made a state entry into Isái, with all the pomp and circumstance which could be mustered for the occasion. Indeed the display was extremely picturesque.

Friday, 22nd January.—HALTED. Post in this morning. Only 6 days, up to 28th December.

Nearly all day trying to make certain about routes to Khárán.

Panjgúr has seen certain vicissitudes since visited by Macgregor and Lockwood in 1877. In the same year the Náoshírwánís came down from

Kharán and succeeded in taking Isái and its fort. Mír Gájián was then absent, having gone with the Khán to the Delhi assemblage and not yet returned. His second brother was killed in the fighting, and in a month or six weeks the Naoshirwánís had got possession of every place in the valley except Sordú, where Mír Gájián's little castle held out to the end and was never taken.

In 1878 the Khán sent a force to reinstate Mír Gájián. This was accomplished after a good deal of desultory fighting. The Gitchkís say that there were skirmishes in the palm groves and enclosures of Isái for 9 days before the Náoshirwánís were ousted, but the loss on either side seems to have been but small.

Náoróz Khán, Azad Khán's eldest son (now virtually Mír of Kháran) hastened down with a force, and offered battle, which was declined. After a time the Naoshirwánís, not caring to knock their heads against strongly garrisoned walls, marched back again, leaving Mír Morád Khán who owns land in Panjgúr, to hold the fort which had been built during the year of occupation on the plain north of Khudabadín.

As soon as Naoróz Khán had departed, the Khán's troops sallied forth and invested the fort, which was besieged in a sort of a way for upwards of a year, that is until December 1881. The Naoshirwánís having eaten all their provision, then came to terms, but Mír Morád retains possession of the fort and holds no communication with the Gitchkís. Mír Gájían has for the moment peaceable possession of his district. He transmits Rs. 12,000 a year to the Khán's treasury, and also pays and provides for the garrison of Kalát troops. After this but little remains for himself. However, he enjoy the honour and comfort of ruling his own country; while it is probably more profitable to the Khan to receive, as now, a fixed revenue without trouble, than was formerly the case when the remittances varied from Rs. 35,000 to nothing, and the district was constantly disturbed. (See also Miles' Report.)

It should be understood that Mír Gájián's position is that of a feudatory chief rather than that of a Governor. He informed me he was of Rájpút origin, not Sikh as stated in the Gazetteer, and seemed proud of the fact.

With regard to Miles' remark that the trade with Urmára (in 1873) had increased in proportion as that with Kalat had fallen off, this state of things is now reversed, and the Kalát trade is by far the most considerable. There are no baunias resident here now, but many come at the harvest times to transact business.

The principal, if not the only, article of export is dates. Wheat is imported in exchange. There is abundance of water here but very little land, and what there is, is almost entirely occupied by date groves, under which crops are raised, sometimes in shade so thick that it is surprising how they can ripen. The jowari of this place is of excellent quality, finer than that of Sind.

Returned the Sirdar's visit; he has a defensible house or, Mírí a short distance from the fort. One wife and establishment here and one at Sordú.

At Isái (or Mírí Isa) there is a sort of branch of palm groves, cultivation, and huts, stretching away from the Kaur, south east, for a mile or more. It is called Kahan (not Káhan). The best camping ground for troops would be west of this, and south of Isái, on a large level plain of fine gravel mixed with sand.

Saturday, 23rd January.—HALTED. Survey and routes

Sunday 24th January.— HALTED. Routes the whole day. The following information was obtained regarding Kháárán. To the east of Kháráu town is a string of hamlets, Huráo (6 miles), Gwazagí (7 miles), Miskání Kalát (9 miles). Beyond these are Jodáí Kalát, Kanderáo, Sirés, Dhanóh and Taghap. The latter is somewhat to the south. Gwazagí and Miskání Kalát, or Miskán, seem to be the only ones of any size except Tagháp. They have 50 or 60 huts a piece. Taghap 60 or 70, the rest 20 or 30. Inhabitants are mostly Rakshánís, and they own the land, but the Náoshirwánís own the water (from bands,) and take a share of the produce.

West by south of Kharan town,—two camels stages (about 36 miles),—is Khurmagáí; a new village. Here is some khushkawa cultivation, a small fort, and collection of shepherds huts.

North east, about 10 or 12 miles, is Sáráwán a Kambarání village of about 60 huts. The principal men are Sáiad Khán and Khán Mahomed. The land by rights belongs to the Khan of Kalát, but A'zád Khán enjoys the revenues, and the people obey his rule and join his forces.* It is watered by canals from the Bado which draw off all the water. The dry bed of the river passes close to Khárán on the east.

The pastoral tribes, from the south up to Khárán, are mostly Mahomed Hasánís. They pay "malia" to Isúf Khán of Jibrí, but obey A'zád Khán and join his standard in war.

South east, 6 or 7 miles from the town (always known as A'zád Khán's "shahr" or "Kalát," Khárán being the name of the extensive plain in which it stands), is the hamlet of Gazi containing some 30 or 40 huts of ghuláms.

Náoróz Kalát is two marches north-north east of Khárán town, the intermediate halt being at Sáráwán. Reports differ as to its distance from the latter place, but it is probably 17 or 18 miles. Close by, on the west, is a high hill marked on the map of Macgregor and Lockwood's exploration. The fort stands on high ground, and is considered strong, but is not large. There is some cultivation, an orchard and date trees. The whole is watered by three cuts from the Bado.

Náoróz Kalát, is in Kambárání country, but the inhabitants are ghulams of A'zád Khán.

Wáshuk appears to be 35 to 40 miles east, or east by south, of Badú Rég on the Máshkél. It is 12 marches (about 154 miles) north northeast of Panjgur; and 7 marches (about 94 miles) south west of Khárán town. It is described as situated in the gap of a range of hills † through which the Wáshuk Kaur passes. In general characteristics it resembles one of the Panjgúr villages, or rather probably Gajar. Its huts, fields, and date groves, lie along both sides of the kaur, and in size it is rather larger than Sordu, i. e. about 300 houses. The fort is situated exactly like that of Gwarjak and is of about the same size.‡ There are no resident banias though many go there in the harvest time. Eight or ten blacksmiths live at Wáshuk.

The dates of Wáshuk are excellent, better even than those of Panjgúr.

The inhabitants are Halozí and and Wáshukí Kalandaránís, the principal men being Mir Zangin Halozí, Sultán Mahomed Malikzáda (Sáiad) Khudadád Washukí, and Karam Sháh Halozí. The duties of Naib are entrusted to a

---
* Sáráwán only furnishes 30 men. The population of this place is a floating one, the people going to and from Kalát and other places.
† The Wáshuk range goes east as far as Gréshak on the Soráni route, (No. XII.), but only a short distance in the opposite direction.
‡ There is only a small guard of half a dozen men.

family of three brothers who appear to have equal authority. Their names are Alabaksh, A'oghán and Dúrak.

It is supposed Washúk can turn out 200 to 400 fighting men according to whether the season has been good or bad, for in the latter case a portion of the people remove with their flocks to some more favoured spot.

The revenue of Washúk is $\frac{1}{10}$th of the produce according to the common rule in these parts. It is said there is no inam land. Compare Haji Abdul Nabi.*

Monday, 26th January.—Halted.

Still waiting for camels but plenty to do in the way of routes and surveying.

Tasp is the largest of the Panjgur townships, containing about 600 huts of Mulázais. I'sai has 500 huts, Sordú 250. Khudabádán was formerly thickly inhabited but there are now only about 60 or 70 huts of Amíráris. The date groves are extensive, extending in places to nearly a mile back from the river bed on either side. The cultivation is all among and under the date trees.

At Sorwán to the south-west is only khushkawa cultivation, and no one lives there permanently; the cultivators are Mulázais of Tasp.

Rode out to A'zád Khán's fort north of the east end of Khudábádán. It is only a few hundred yards from the edge of the date groves, and is rudely built of mud and katcha brick, but the walls are high and thick (6 to 8 feet) and in tolerable repair, so it is strong according to Baluch notions. We could not enter it, or even approach very close, as it was still held by Mír Morád Naoshírwání. The walls are certainly 20 feet high, and the perimeter probably under 200 yards, measured outside. It is of irregular trace with a square tower. There is a well inside.

Khudábádán was given by Nasír Khan 1st to A'zád Khán's father or grandfather in inám. Under present circumstances of course he gets nothing out of it, but Mír Morád Khán, who has some of the land, is said to be allowed to enjoy the proceeds.

A post in this evening.

Tuesday, 27th January.—Halted.

Camels came in last night, but the owners want to make their own terms and the Sirdar is settling with them.

To-day and the last two days have been cold, with a strong north wind, making the atmosphere as usual very hazy and dirty. This weather is a remarkable contrast to the heat of the first day or two.

There are said to be no internal dissensions in Panjgúr now. The revenue as is generally customary in these parts, is $\frac{1}{10}$th of all produce, and that is paid to Mír Gajíán cheerfully enough.

To continue notes on villages in Khárán. The most important place in the country, next to A'zád Khán's town, and ranking above Wáshúk, is Kalag. This is a group of 9 hamlets lying along a stream called the Chihaltánání Kaur, disposed much as in Panjgúr and similar places.

The names of the villages are as follows:—

(1) Erí Kalát, (2) Nardután, (3) Razai, (4) Kalshinán, (5) Garók, (6) Patinúk, (7) Máladín, (8) Lús, (9) Chihaltáu; (3) and (6) are on the left bank of the kaur, all the others on the right.

---
* It may be as well to remark here that I had Háji Abdul Nabi's account of his journey with me, and compared it with the statements of the Panjgur people to many of whom Khárán and Wáshúk are well known. I also asked them leading questions from the book. It will be noticed that in some important particulars the Háji's report is not confirmed.

Erí is 17 or 18 miles north-west or west-north-west of Khárán town. There are wells on the road. From Erí to Chihaltán is 10 miles. The hamlets are individually small, Kalshinán, the largest, having only 30 or 40 huts. That is, I understand, *permanent* habitations. The kaur runs south or south-south-east to Gwásh, which is the open plain south of Khárán and is there dissipated. About the villages there is a fair amount of cultivation irrigated from the kaur, also small date groves, orchards and vines. The people are Sáhpád Rinds. Their chief Núr Muhamad lives at Kalshinán and another wahdera, Rústam, at Máládín. The Sápád furnish 500 men to the Khárán forces, of whom 300, or thereabouts, come from Kalag.

Since the invasion of Khárán by the Khán of Kalát (in 1858?,) at which time Kalag fell into the hands of the Kalát army, a new fort has been built on another kaur which runs parallel to, and 8 or 10 miles east of, the Chihaltánáni. It is called Jhálawár. There is a high hill east of the fort, between it and the stream; another to the south-west, and a third to the north-west. The spurs of these unite, forming a circle of hills, about 1000 yards in diameter, in the midst of which the fort is situated.* On the peaks are strong towers and a good deal of labour is said to have been expended in making the position as strong as possible. As the ridges are described as being high and scarped, and in many places inaccessible, it is possible the position may be formidable, but the Baluch have no genius for fortification.† It is acknowledged that the hills once taken the fort itself could make but little resistance. Such as it is, however, this is A'zád Khán's stronghold, and here he himself resides with his family. His treasure is also kept here. The permanent garrison of Jhálawár is not less than 500 muskets. There is a well in the fort, but the water is not good, and drinking water is generally obtained from the stream or springs on the east.

Some 3 or 4 miles to the north is a range through which the kaur comes and east of the gap is a conspicuous peak called Mamú.

A'zád Khán's frontier is the Hajbdfáh range and other hills forming the northern boundary of Panjgúr; westwards the line goes to the Gráwag Tank,‡ where they say Khárán, Jalk, and Panjgúr all join. Kuhak belongs to Khárán.

There are 5 or 6 blacksmiths in Panjgúr; one carpenter and mill-wright, (this man is a Sikh and lives at Sordú); also ten moochees.

The climate of Panjgúr is admitted to be decidedly unhealthy in summer, and appears to be relaxing at all times. My men complained of the water, but it is apparently sweet and good. Stone in the bladder is said to occur occasionally in the valley.

Mír Gajúan can muster in his district 1,500 fighting men, of whom about 150 are mounted. Almost every man carries a shield in this country.

There are no watermills now in Panjgúr though there were formerly. The Sirdar, however, has a bullock mill at Isai which grinds for the detachment of Khán's troops. With relays of bullocks it is supposed to be capable of turning out 8 to 10 maunds of flour in 24 hours.

Wednesday, 28th January.—SHA'HBA'Z KALA'T. Elevation 4,055 feet, 25 miles. (By the Sháhmí Kand).

---

* The east hill is the nearest. The others are ¾rd of a mile distant.

† The place mentioned as "Kalling" (an impossible name) in No. XVI. of the routes attached to "Biluchistán," by A. W. Hughes, F. R. G. S., is no doubt the same.

‡ See also Macgregor's "Wanderings in Biluchistán."

From Isai south-east. At about 1 mile pass the last palm trees. Soon after the low conglomerate bluffs of the central plateau trend back, and the track crosses an extensive gravelly plain. Broad, but very shallow, watercourses, grown with pish, run from left to right to join the kaur below Isai.

After 5 miles the ascent becomes perceptible. "Dámán" strewn with dark coloured fragments of trap rock, but track good.

At about 7 miles enter the hills.

A water-course is followed for a short distance, and the road, ascending left bank, crosses a bent or small plateau.

At about 8 miles descend again to the watercourse, and cross it. There is then a short and slightly rough ascent to low broken hills through which the road passes. These are part of the second range, which is at some distance from the third range. Intervening ground a long strip of partly open barren country cut by deep water-courses and broken by small hills.

At about 9 miles the nala is again entered, and now followed through a short gorge in a tolerably high range of metamorphic rock. Here, at 9 miles, is water, called (I think) Kashindar. It is abundant and good, but there is no place to camp. The nala, after passing the hills, is followed round to the east for a short distance, and then south. It now becomes very narrow, and is a defile sunk among a mass of inferior clay slate hills between the third range and main ridge.

Up to this point the road is good, but at about 10 miles the track takes to the hill side on the right, there being an impassable place a little higher up. The path is very narrow, and there is a steep fall of 40 to 50 feet to the torrent bed, into which an animal would be precipitated on making a false step.

After a quarter of a mile or so the nala is regained by a steep, rocky and awkward descent.

After a short distance a small rocky spur, between narrow ravines, is ascended. The path is very fair and the clay slate affords good foothold.

Beyond this is a short and easy ascent to the crest of the pass, which is reached at 11½ miles. Elevation 5150 feet. A good view is obtainable here over Panjgúr to the north, and the Gwárgu valley to south.

The descent is steep and rough, more difficult than the ascent, and the gradient for the first few hundred yards is probably not less than 1 in 7 or 1 in 8. From thence down a gradually widening, and winding, ravine; general direction south-east coming round to south-west. At 3½ miles from the crest (15 miles), after a rather long westerly bend, the last low range is past and the Gwárgu valley entered.

About S. S. W. from here, 4 to 5 miles across the valley, is a well called Pakúálí said to contain a good supply of water. It is on one of the tracks to the Gandagarók Kand, which is reported practicable for horsemen.

Gwárgú, as before mentioned, is a continuation of Gitchk and separated from it only by a watershed. It is about 4 miles wide, and extends west to the Pulábád plain* in which Shahbáz Kalát is situated. It is drained by two very broad and shallow water courses, thickly grown with tamarisk, and the whole

---

* Pulábád is a village in the plain a short march west of Shahbáz Kalát. Here are 200 huts of Talúkáni, Dashti and Barak Balúch, ryots of Mir Gajián. There are many wells and water is abundant. Formerly there were 2 karezes, but they have long been choked and the land is now only khushkáwa. Many camels are grazed in this country. From Pulábád there is a road to Kej:—

(1) Miták Sing, (2) Kamar, (3) Kambur Glar, (4) Jubelar, (5) Gazbasan, (6) Shaitáp, (7) Boleda, (8) Garók (hamésap), (9) Gokpr sh, (10) Jadgál (beyond kand of the same name,) (11) Kej.

The above are all camel stages and short marches. The road is tolerable, but not so good as the ordinary one, and no shorter. Moreover it has not the same advantages in the way of wood, water and camel grazing

valley is well covered with low shrubs and grass, presenting a decided contrast to the excessive barenness of Panjgúr, outside of the fertile strip along the kaur. The inhabitants of Gwárgú seem to be a Mingal section. They are raiats of Mír Gajíán. From the exit of the Sháhmí Pass to Sháhbáz Kalát is about 10 miles in a straight line. There is no road, but the way cannot be mistaken and the travelling is easy.

Sháhbáz Kalát is a rude fort situated on a mound on the south side of a plain of alluvial soil mixed with sand. It is commanded by low hills at four or five hundred yards to the south-east, but that is of no consequence in Baluch warfare. It is in good repair. The walls are about 10 feet high with small square towers. The trace is irregular, adapted to the site, and the perimeter about 100 yards. The entrance is on the west side. There are two wells, without, at the base of the mound. One is about 75 feet deep, the other 40 feet. Good supply of water in both. Some 700 or 800 yards south-west is a third well. At present Mír Gájíán has a garrison of 20 men in the fort.

The plain is somewhat cut up with water-courses. There is a good deal of tolerable khushkáwa land, but we saw none under cultivation. The people are Kasháni Balúch, raiats of Mír Gajíán. They can muster altogether about 200 fighting men.

On the east, the plain adjoins Gwárgú, of which it practically forms a part. West it stretches an indefinite distance, and the country appears very open in that direction. North, about 4 miles, are the Kasháni hills separating the plain from that of Panjgúr, and south are the ranges through which lies the road to Kílkaur, Kólwah, Urmára, and Kej. Water, wood, camel grazing, and grass abundant. Ample ground for encampment.

From Sháhbáz Kalát to Isai is about 21 miles by the Kasháni road which is the straightest and best. The range is crossed by a pass so easy that it is little more than a watershed. However to gain this a slight detour is made. On the straight road is a small kand, but it is easy. Kafilas halt at Mántar* about half way. Here is a rather scanty supply of water in the bed a nala, a few hundred yards east of the road. Moreover there appears to be but little room for encampment.†

Between the Kasháni road and Sháhmí Kand is a pass called Nakíbo. By it there is a good camel road, but it joins the Kasháni route within the hills on the Panjgúr side, and is longer than the latter so there is no advantage in taking it.

Thursday, 29th January,—ZAM. Elevation 4120 feet. 19 miles. South-west from the fort, passing third well at a short half mile. The track is heavy in sand to within the first hills. At the well bend south-south-west; at $2\frac{1}{2}$ miles pass first hills, a broken range of trap dyke. Passing through low detached rocks, a stony and gravelly undulating plain is entered. It extends far to the west.

At $5\frac{1}{4}$ miles pass through low hills and hillocks. The road is good, but there is a perceptible ascent all the way from Sháhbáz Kalát.

At about 6 miles a drop of 15 feet into a nala. No difficulty for laden animals.

The main range is now approached and entered at about 8 miles. The path, following a small water course, ascends for a short half mile to a low

---

* This name, Mántar or Mánchar, is very common, and means a loop or bend, as of a stream.
† See also Macgregor's " Wanderings in Biluchistan."

kotal, called Ziruuk. It is a little rough, but the gradient is good, and the hills on either hand of no height, and easily accessible. They are of the usual clay slate and trap.

There are two tracks over the kotal. That to right (west) is perhaps a little the best.

Descent easy, but longer than the ascent.

At about 9¼ miles the road drops into a deep watercourse, at the edge of which is a small road side ziárat.

This is the Wash Jaurkán Nála. It runs westward and then north, joining the stream of Panjgúr, afterwards known as the Máshkel.

The tract now entered is a narrow broken valley; about 2 miles in front is a range similar to that first passed and running parallel to it east and west.

The road turns east up the watercourse which is about 25 yards across between high banks. Following the nála it turns south-west and just beyond, at 11 miles, are shallow rock pools. Here is Wash Jaurkán halting-place.

The camping ground would be on conglomerate plateaux on left bank, either above or below water. There is very little room on the right bank. All the available ground is commanded from the north by accessible hills of moderate height.

The bed of the nála is thickly grown with coarse grass, oleander, and písh. *Gurkao* grass, which is better than *barshón*, is abundant in the neighbourhood; also camel grazing. Wood moderate. Water abundant, but slightly saline.

Wash is "sweet," and jaurkán "oleander." There is one of the usual legends, to the effect that a man arrived here in a starving condition and implored the Pír buried in the ziárat abovementioned for assistance in the shape of food. After this he felt impelled to eat the oleander blossoms, and to his surprise found them sweet and nourishing.

From Wash Jaurkán water the track ascends a small side ravine. On the left hand is a hole in the conglomerate bank. It is said to have been made by a Persian force camped here during one of their invasions, and was intended for the storage of their powder during heavy rain, which occurred at that time.

The road goes east for about 2 miles, and then bends east-south-east, crossing the valley diagonally through low hills and broken ground. At 3½ miles is a watershed, the drainage beyond going to the Kil Kaur, and so to Kej. Height 3,325 feet.

Thence the track descends a nála, at first very small and narrow, and sunk between clay slate banks. Road good.

At 5 miles is a little water, the head of that called Mántar. There would be room to camp above the bank, and kafilas sometimes halt here.* The nála is still very narrow and the road for a short distance not so good. At about 6 miles pass, still following the watercourse, through the first ridge in the Istarag range. Here a ledge of rocks crossing the nála bed makes the road rough for a few yards. There is perennial water at this spot.

From hence the road for about 3 miles lies through a winding defile or gorge between rather lofty and bold hills of the usual formation. Although nothing very grand, this defile is a relief from the barren monotony of the endless clay slate and trap ridges of which this country entirely consists. It is called Mántar (or Manchar), a word meaning loop, or bend, as of a stream, and of common occurrence. Water is constant for about two-thirds of the

and it is sweet and good. The descent is rapid, probably 1 in 20 to 1 in 25, and the road, over clay slate gravel, is mostly good. There are, however, one or two rough bits, where the bed rocks crop up, and at one spot cavalry might have to dismount.*

At 9 miles the mouth of the defile is reached. Here, on the left hand side going down, is a small waterhole, and as the nála is called Zám after issuing from the hills, this is known to kafila people as the Zám halting place. There is no room to camp any but the smallest detachment. We pitched north of the water, which is sweet, but rather scanty. Grass and fuel abundant. Camel grazing scanty. The hills to east are called Janakajík.

Troops would never halt here. Garak on the same nála, 5 miles on, is a much better place.

This is Sájdí or Sáka country. It is in the Panjgúr district.

Road generally good. Minimum of thermometer last night 28.°

Friday, 30th January.—Kíl Kaur (salt nála) 20½ miles. Elevation 2,010 feet.

Follow the nála, now called Zám (*sicord*). At 1¼ miles road ascends to the right bank, and a quarter of a mile further it is joined by the track from Mántar over the Istarag Kand. This path cuts off the Mántar windings, but the pass is difficult.

The tract now traversed is a broken country of small ridges and pfsh grown nálas, the latter running southwards. The road is either in, or near, the Zúm. It is good. At 4½ miles the nála passes through the next range, a single one, much inferior in height to those on either side of the Mántar defile. That part on the left (east) of the gap is the Zám Kóh. Here, where the nála enters the hills, the road is joined by the Gandagarók track. This path goes north, nearly straight over the hills, into Gwárgú, from which it is continued in the same line by the Sháhmi Kand road into Panjgúr.

The Gandagarók Kand is high, but, it is said, not very steep. It is, however, impracticable for laden camels.† It is rather better than the Sháhmi Kand, and could no doubt be easily made into a fair road if worth while. The halting place in Gwárgú is at Sámán, where there is an old fort and apparently some khushkáwa land. Water runs in the Gwárgú Kaur down to this point, which is somewhat to the right of the direct line. Wood, grass, and camel grazing abundant. Distance from Sámán to Chetkán in Panjgúr 18 or 19 miles.

No doubt this road saves a good deal of ground, especially if the journey is to be continued towards Kháran by the Hajhdiár Pass, but where large numbers of baggage animals are concerned, camels especially, the road with the easiest gradients will prove the shortest in the long run.

At 5 miles water reappears in the bed of the Zám. There is a fine pool under a rock, and the water is said to run from hence continuously to the Kíl Kaur. Good ground for encampment below the pool on both sides of the nála. Grass moderate; camel grazing moderate; wood abundant. Unfortunately the water is decidedly saline, but it is good enough for one night. Country around half open, with two broken ridges.

The proper name of this place is Garak, but it is evidently the "Zahm" of Miles.

---

* The Mántar defile, as might be expected, is occasionally rendered impassable by floods. But it is asserted by all that these only occur in summer. The winter rain is mild.

† Very conflicting statements were made to us about this pass. One individual asserted that it was impossible to ride over it. I believe the truth to be as stated above.

From the pool the road goes for a few hundred yards along the right bank, and then crosses to left. Thence it runs along a smooth level plain or plateau with low hills on the left hand (east.)

Here we met a kafila of 27 camels from Urára for Panjgút with wheat, rice, sugar, dried fish, and stuffs.

At 7 miles again enter the hills, crossing a small easy kotal. The descent is into a nála running west to the Zám, now about a mile on the right. The latter goes away into the hills and is no more seen. It joins the Kíl Kaur.

Here is a sort of hollow or narrow irregular valley. To south it is bounded by a considerable range called Nap or Napta. The round turns left (east) under the ridge just passed. At first there is a slight ascent and then a descent to regain the watercourse, known as the Napta Sham (Nafta Sham of Lockwood). It is entered at 8 miles, and followed for a short distance. Here we met another kafila of 10 camels bound for Panjgúr from Kej.

Thence through low hills to an almost imperceptible watershed gained at 8½ miles. Here a bend to the right and descent southwards down a small clay slate ravine, one of the heads of the Gúmbak. It is very narrow, only a yard or two wide, and the turns are exceedingly sharp. Road very good.

After half a mile a more open tract is entered, and the road quits the watercourse to left, crossing a small plain amidst low hills. In front is another considerable range, the Gúmbak Koh.

At 9¼ miles descend into the Gúmbak Kaur, a large watercourse. At 10 miles the Mádag road branches to the left (east.)

This village (in the Kolwáh plain) is said to be only 10 or 12 miles distant.* The road is a tolerable one and used by kafilas, but the Mádag Kand over the last high range seems to be rather difficult. There are five kotals, of which two have a steep side, one north and one south. Mádag belongs to Kaodai Balúch (Dost Muhammad Khán), but the people have been driven, thence by Balúch Khán Naoshírwání of Hor, and have taken refuge in Gwarkóp.

At 10¼ miles water appears in the Gúmbak. It is plentiful and sweet and runs for about a quarter of a mile, but there does not appear to be any place to pitch a camp. On either side are the Gúmbak hills, but they hardly approach close enough to make a defile.

When the last water is passed the Gúmbak hills are also quitted, and shortly afterwards the nála bears away to the left, the road keeping pretty straight on, and descending through low hills over dámán of the usual description. At about 12¼ miles is a long narrow plain called Karpala. The west end only is crossed. It extends some miles to the east, and there is there a certain amount of good alluvial soil; the first seen since quitting Shábáz Kalát 30 miles back. The Gúmbak Nála, its course marked by a line of low trees, crosses Karpala about two miles east of the road, and its flood water is sometimes utilised for cultivation, but the country seems to be too unsettled for agriculture.†

Beyond Karpala the road traverses low hills; then a very small strip of plain, and at 14 miles there is a slight descent through hills to the wooded plan of Dashtak.

This is of considerable size, being about 1½ miles across, and stretching several miles both east and west. In the former direction it is divided longi-

---

* This is absurd. [illegible] he at least 30 miles, see note, page 67.
† Meshkai Kumb is a [illegible] korsala. L kwe Isays it never dries up, but according to the guides there is no water this season. We [illegible] as it was half a mile to east of the road, but as the guides were doing all they could to induce us to make short marches, I believe their statement on this occasion.

tudinally by a ridge. People here are Sájdís, living by their flocks. They also make attempts at cultivation as the rainfall and their enemies may permit. There is no surface water either in Dashtak or Karpala except rain-pools. No doubt it could easily be got by digging, as abundant grass and vegetation show that it exists at no great depth.

On entering Dashtak the road forks. The left hand branch is the proper direct route. The other leads to Rekunah, and so, by a rather roundabout but easy way, to the Kolwáh plain. As the divergence is at first but small, one path may easily be mistaken for the other.

(As it happened, our baggage did take the wrong road, but this was a piece of wilfulness on the part of the guide. We did not overtake it till it got to Rekunah 3½ miles on; and as I wanted to see the road, we had to retrace our steps to Dashtak, thus adding over 5 miles to the march.)

Crossing the Dashtak plain, the hills are again entered at 15½ miles, and the road winds through them, keeping pretty much on a level. It bends decidedly to the left or south-east.

At about 17¼ miles cross the Kaur Tor, a broad, rough watercourse.

At 18 miles enter a high range of hills called Ginkash. This is a double range, bare and rugged. The first ridge is passed with only a slight ascent and descent. Road fair. The second ascent terminates in a rather steep rise to a kand, the crest of which is gained at 18 miles. The descent is much greater. It is nearly straight, steep and somewhat rough. At the top it is also very narrow.

Below is a gravelly plain with small trees and bushes, over which the road is good.

At 19¾ miles begin again to descend and pass through small hills. We halted on the further side of these at 20½ miles in a sort of rough and jungly valley, lying as usual east and west, but sloping to the south. About a mile east of the road the Gúmbak joins a kaur, apparently known as the Lesser Kíl and we camped on the latter. Its water is so salt as to be almost undrinkable and it was again a piece of misconduct on the part of the guides not to take us on to the real Kíl Kaur, 1½ miles further. It was in fact nearly 8 o'clock, we had been marching about 11 hours, and they were tired.

Road to-day good—better than yesterday. High northerly winds since leaving Panjgúr. The decrease in elevation seems to make but little difference in the temperature. The nights are cold, and the days by no means hot.

The road to Rekunah is as follows: From where Dashtak is entered at 3½ miles from Gúmbak, take the right hand track, which diverges at first but slightly from the other.

At 4 miles pass the end of the longitudinal ridge dividing the western end of Dashtak. At 4¾ miles again enter hills. Here is another and very small strip of plain. The road bends south-west and then west.

At 5¾ miles another ridge is reached and crossed by a low kotal.

The road still keeping away to the west crosses another and higher kotal at 6¼ miles.

Descent is into a rather deep ravine, the head of the Rekunah Nála. The bottom is narrow, but good travelling. It is followed first west and then south. At 7 miles, a few yards off the road to the left (east), is a small running stream. This is the kafila halting place called Rekunah. Water is abundant, and probably grass also. Wood and camel grazing moderate or scanty. Distance from Garak about 12¼ miles.

As the sun had now set, and 8 or 9 miles of road still lay before us, it was impossible to examine this place properly, but there did not appear to be any room to form an encampment. The valley or ravine is sunk among considerable heights, and the camp lies under a high hill to south, which is part of the Ginkash range, and visible from Dashtak. The nála runs west under this, and then appears to turn south through the range. It joins the Kíl Kaur. There is said to be an easy cross track from here to Kíl Kaur; but I choose to go back to Dashtak for the reason above stated. Fortunately a good moon enabled the country to be observed nearly as well as by daylight.

From Rekunah the route is said to lead as follows:—

(1) Mahabúr 14 or 15 miles, passing half way a place called Tétagár, where kafilas occasionally halt.

(2) Balúr about the same distance.

This route is longer than the one followed, but is said to be easier, and it turns the Hodál Pass.

Saturday, 31st January.—BALÚR. 21½ miles. Elevation 914 feet.

From our camp on the Kíl Kaur salt stream, enter the hills almost immediately, and cross a low neck. The stream goes through a gap, a short distance to left (east). Short and easy descent to the Kíl Kaur valley. It is thickly wooded with large tamarisk and babul trees.

At 1½ miles turn south-east and cross the Kíl Kaur, a large watercourse, running between moderately high banks of soft alluvial soil. Water in long pools; crossing easy. Beyond is a good open plain fit for encampment. Water abundant and good. Wood, grass, and camel grazing also abundant. Distance from Garak (Zám Nála) 17 miles. This is about the best halting place on the whole road, and would be a convenient spot for a depôt, or for troops to remain a day and rest their transport.*

From here road leads south-east across the plain, slightly rising and becoming stony after a short distance.

At about 3 miles pass through an outer ridge of the high hills lying in front. Thence a mile of steady ascent (probably 1 in 30) over tolerably smooth *dámán*. At 4 miles the road, following a watercourse, traverses low hills at the foot of the main range. After this another half mile or more of *dámán*. Ascent about 1 in 25.

At about 4¾ miles descend again into the nála and follow it up into the hills. At 5¼ miles enter a narrow gorge, wild and rugged, continually ascending between clay slate heights 300 to 400 feet high. They are steep, but accessible. Road in the bed of the torrent is rather rough, but quite practicable for laden camels.

The ascent grows steeper and steeper, till it becomes from 1 in 15 to 1 in 12. Here the ravine is very narrow, only a few feet wide at bottom.

At about 6 miles leave the ravine, and turning to the right ascend a smooth well marked path up a sort of cleft to the crest of the pass. This bit is 1 in 4 or 1 in 5, and over 100 yards long. It is barely wide enough for a laden camel to get up.

The crest of this pass, called the Hodál Kand, is not a ridge, but comparatively wide and open, sloping to south. Elevation about 3,150 feet, or some 1,200 feet above the Kíl Kaur valley. To the north is a long, but not extensive, view. Janakajik, to east of the Mántar defile, and the Gandagarók Kand

---

* The Kíl Kaur, like other hill streams, is liable to heavy floods, but these rarely, if ever, occur except at intervals, and subside so quickly, that travellers are only detained for a night or so.

are plainly visible. There is no outlook southwards from the pass itself. The crest of the range is the boundary between the Panjgúr and Kólwáh districts.

The descent as to gradient is easy. It lies down a narrow ravine, which is a little rough for the first few yards.

As the nála is descended, the heights on either hand naturally become greater. At about a mile from the crest the ravine leads into a larger one. This is called Nághai, which is also the name of the range, or at least this portion of it. Here is water in several places.

The Nághai ravine soon becomes 50 or 60 yards broad, and widens gradually. It is pretty thickly grown with tamarisk and písh, but has a wide smooth water channel, down which is an excellent track over slaty gravel, rather soft than otherwise.

The gradient here is probably about 1 in 30. Hills clay slate, and high, but accessible. The pass winds somewhat, but not much.

At 10½ miles (4½ from crest) leave the high hills rather abruptly. Here the path to Nág branches to right (south-west). That place is rather more than a mile distant. It was visited by Lockwood, who calls it Nál, possibly a misprint. Miles gives the name correctly. We were informed that there is a hamlet there, with a small fort and some cultivation,* which Lockwood does not mention.

The road goes straight on down the nála, here 150 yards wide, between high sloping banks. About a mile further (5½ from crest of Hodál) and right in the kaur is a thin clump of date trees and tiny patches of cultivation. This is Kuldán ; it is watered by a good spring, and there would be tolerable ground for encampment on the low plateaux (dámán) adjacent to the nála. There are no permanent inhabitants here. The place belongs to Dost Muhammad Kaodai of Mádag, but he and his people have been driven thence by Balúch Khán Naoshírwání of Hor, and with their clansmen of Balúr have taken refuge in Gwarkóp.

Distance from Kíl Kaur proper 10 miles. Mádag is about 16 miles from Kuldán, nearly due east.

Wood, water, and camel grazing appear tolerably abundant at Kuldán, grass doubtful.

Here we passed a donkey kafila from Urmára carrying dried fish to Panjgúr.

Immediately to south of Kuldán is a low outer range of some thickness through which the kaur passes. The road lies in the bed of the watercourse and is good. At 1 mile pass waterholes. At 2 miles the hills are left, but their dámán continues, and it is another mile to where the nála fairly debouches on the plain.

But before this it is quitted, the track bending somewhat to left (east) and descending the gentle gravelly slope. The Kolwáh plain now lies in front, stretching east-north-east as far as the eye can reach. On the west it adjoins that of Kej, being only divided therefrom by a watershed, said to be a march distant.† The breadth of the plain, including dámán on both sides, is about 7 miles. The ranges beyond (south) appear rather low from the plain. There is, however, a high hill to south-west called Girdánk, which is visible from the

* About 25 huts of Kaodai Balúch, malik Khuda Baksh. There is a karez with a date grove and a little irrigated land. Khuda Baksh lives in the fort, which is not on a mound or elevation. It has one tower. A certain quantity of barley can generally be procured here.
† Ross travelled over this and also Lockwood.

neighbourhood of Urmára. At 4 miles the track strikes alluvial soil, and shortly afterwards passes a ruinous fort on a mound. This is Gat. There is plenty of good khushkáwa land about here, and some is now under cultivation. It belongs to the people of Nág. The fort is inhabited in summer. At the south base of the mound is a well. The people hereabouts are Nághai Balúch.

The portion of the Kólwáh plain now traversed is called Rodakán. It is rather well wooded along this, its northern, side. Tamarisk is the principal tree, or rather bush, and the vegetation is that of a low country, láni, ak, (milky euphorbia), drab grass, and so forth. There is no irrigated land.

In the centre of the plain is more cultivation, and having passed this, the track suddenly disappears at about 7 miles. Guides, however, make for a well known gap in the hills through which the road passes. From Gat the track has been south or south-south-east; a decided turn to the left is now made, and a line taken south-east or east-south-east. The plain is here almost bare, except for low scrub and thick tussocks of drab grass.

At 10 miles leave alluvial soil and ascend a very gently sloping, smooth *dámán*. The path now reappears, and is well marked.

At 10¾ miles descend into a nála, which is crossed. Thence ascend steadily through low hills. Good road. At 12½ miles cross watershed called the Kúnerí Kand. Gradients on both sides easy.

Thence descend a watercourse bending round to the right (south). The hills are everywhere low, broken, and easily accessible.

At 13 miles from Kuldán reach Balúr. Here is a small plantation of young date trees, surrounded as usual by a thin fence of palm branches, and watered by a small stream in several rills. No one living here now except two men in charge of the plantation. The people (Kaodai Baltich, Ibráhím Khán) have, as before stated, fled to Gwarkóp to escape from their enemies, the Naoshírwánís of Hor.

Camping ground, at the water, confined, and surrounded by low hills. Water tolerably abundant and good. Fuel, grass, and camel grazing scanty, but abundant in the Kólwáh plain 3 miles off.

A road from Mádag comes in here.

Despite the decrease in elevation, it is still cold, and we did not experience the difference in temperature south of the Hodál Pass to which Miles refers. A strong northerly wind was probably the cause. Minimum of thermometer this night 26°. About the same as at Panjgúr, which is nearly 2,000 feet higher.

Sunday, 1st February.—HARÉTRAK. 4 miles. Elevation 2,137 feet.

The camels with our grain and flour not having appeared last night, we were obliged to make a short march to allow them to come up. The guide, lying as usual, said there was no water for a long way beyond Harétrak, and on coming up I found the baggage had been unloaded.

From Balúr south-south-east ascending to a smooth gravel plateau. This would make a good camping ground, and is not too far from the water-supply.

At ¾ of a mile leave the plateau and descend to the Más (*mother*) Balúrí Kaur, and turn up it south-south-west. Low hills on both sides.

At 1¼ miles follow the nála south through a small range, after which it resumes its former westerly direction.

At 2 miles pass a waterhole under the hill on left. A little beyond this climb the hills to left (south) by a rough path narrow at the top. This is the

Balúrí Kand; it leads to an elevated gravel plateau broken by small rocky ridges and detached hills. Over this the road strikes south-south-east.

At 3½ miles cross drainage channel, and shortly afterwards a branch of the same. They run west, and then south, through the hills beyond.

At 4 miles, having approached the ranges bounding the plateau on the south, descend into a small watercourse, which goes to join the main channel.

Here is water, and we camped. It is not a place where troops would remain except of necessity. Water-supply moderate; it is good, though slightly saline. Camel grazing and wood tolerably abundant down the nála. Grass, (putár, &c.), fairly plentiful on the hills.

According to the aneroid, this place is all but 1,200 feet higher than Balúr. It does not seem nearly so much.

The plateau is noticeable as being the watershed between Kólwáh drainage and that which goes *ria* the Siahdád Nála to the Basúl Kaur, and so to the sea. Kólwáh is a basin, and its water has no outlet.

Monday, 2nd February.—ANGIR. 20½ miles. Elevation 615 feet.

From water at first cast, and almost immediately turn south through the first hills to the Dédárí (cactus) Kaur, a broad nála going away eastward. It runs along the base of a considerable range known as the Kahúr Kand Kóh.

At the foot of the same range is a nála going in the opposite direction. This is one of the heads of the Kahúr Kand Kaur. The road bends south-west away from Dédárí, and then west, striking this nála and following it down. I did not observe the watershed, so it must be very slight. High parallel ridges run east and west; the watercourses in the intermediate ravines make their way south through gaps.

At 1½ miles turn south through first Kahúr range, then east.

And 2 miles again south through the second range of Kahúr. After passing this, the kaur goes away eastward. It joins the Dédárí, and both eventually run to the Basúl. The track, however, turns west up an affluent nála. It is rough travelling, the hills having changed from clay slate to sandstone, or metamorphic clay stone. The bed of the torrent is therefore a mass of stones and small boulders instead of the fine soft gravel into which clay slate disintegrates.

All the way from Harétrak the road has been more or less of a defile. The ravine now traversed is not more than 30 yards wide, and is narrower as one advances. The whole country is a mass of parallel ridges, bare and rocky.

At 3 miles the torrent bed is quitted, and the track turning to left (south) crosses an inconsiderable kotal by a narrow path. Beyond is a broader and smoother ravine up which the road turns east. It is good.

This ravine also soon becomes small. At 3½ miles the track ascends northeast to another trifling kotal. These two are the Kahúr Kand. The latter is over a clay slate ridge, and the road good.

Thence eastward down a long narrow ravine. Good road. At about 4½ miles cross a small neck leading to a side ravine. The main nála is left on the right, and becomes impassable. Somewhat high hills on all sides.

At 4½ miles is a descent southwards. There is water at the foot. The same ravine is now followed west-south-west. It is called Kurúchí, and the hills, which are high on both sides, especially to left (south), are the Kurúchí hills.

At 5 miles Kurúchí spring. Good water, but no room to camp. The ravine is narrow all the way, and is here only 6 or 7 yards wide; but the road is good.

At 5½ miles turn south, still following the nála. The Kahúr and Kurúchí hills are now left behind, but the watercourse is still a defile, sunk among inferior ridges. In front, at some distance south-south-east, is the higher range called Síahdád.

At about 6 miles, the road having left the nála (which goes east), turns to west, and thence leads between low clayey ranges. It is good. Girdánk hill appears to be part of the Kurúchí range. It is seen here nearly due west, apparently about 5 miles off, and stands high above everything in the vicinity. It is an excellent landmark and is evidently the peak marked in Macgregor and Lockwood's map. At 7 miles reach a watercourse called Kásag Prúsh, and follow it at first south-south-west. Hills on the left 250 to 300 feet high; those on right (west) quite low.

Miles made his first halt from Balúr in this kaur, and calls the distance 12 miles. There was no water when we passed.

The Kásag Prúsh is followed through low clay hills in a general south-easterly direction for about a mile, when the track leaves it, turning west along small ravine.

This kaur, like the others, goes away eastward.

At 9 miles turn completely round the end of a low ridge from west to east, but soon again following the watercourse to south, and then south-west. Road good all the way.

The kaur now descended is the Síahdád. It is not quitted henceforward until the hills are left 23 miles from Urmára.

At 9¾ miles pass through an outer range of the Síahdád hills. Thence south-west to the main ranges, the inferior ridges of which are entered at 10 miles. This part of the road is fair, but the bed of the nála, of firm set claystone shingle, is not exactly pleasant travelling. Descent very perceptible. At 10¾ miles the broad watercourse turns left (east) under the first main range, and at 11 enters the Síahdád defile.

Here under a rock on the left hand (east) is a rain water pool and kafila halting place. The water dries up in summer, but is now 1½ feet deep, though there has been no rain for more than three months. Sometimes it is 3 or 4 feet deep.

This place (known as Síahdád) is 15 miles from Balúr. There is comparatively open ground to north, but it seems altogether too rough for pitching tents. Troops, however, could bivouac comfortably enough, and the climate here is never very cold.

Wood and camel grazing abundant. Grass apparently scanty, at least in the immediate neighbourhood. Elevation about 1,365 feet.

The range in which the water lies is quickly past, but the highest range of Síahdád is beyond.

The track bends south-east crossing a bent (plateau), and regains nála at half a mile. This bent would make a good camping ground, but is not very near the water.

Thence enter the hills. The defile winds east-south-east, and then east Heights are rocky and steep. The gorge (as far as I can remember) is 40 or 5 yards wide. Track tolerable, over shingle firm set in a bed of clay.

At 1½ miles turn south and quit the Síahdád ranges. The road continues to follow the broad and stony nála southwards, bending with it south-west at 2 miles. Here it lies through clayey hills, steep but not high. Steady descent of about 1 in 30 to 1 in 35 all the way from Síahdád water.

(51)

At 3 miles the hills close in somewhat, narrowing the pass from 300 or 400 yards to 50 or 60.

At 3¼ miles the road bends south-west, crossing a bend, and is very good. On the left (south) is a considerable and rather regular range, the Ábgir Koh. On the right are low hills near the road.

At about 4 miles regain the kaur, here 200 yards across, and proceed along it west. Road good.

Hereabouts is perennial running water, which we unfortunately did not see. It is known as Gorám Bént, from the name of the next plateau (Zorámibeit of Miles). The supply is said to be ample. Wood, camel grazing, and grass abundant. Distance from Balúr 19 to 20 miles; and if Síahdád rainpool failed, this would have to be the halting place.

At 5¼ miles ascend left bank on to the narrow Gorám Bént between the Ábgir Koh and the kaur. It is smooth and level, and would make an excellent camping ground. Road very good.

At 5¾ miles the plateau comes to an end, and the nála is re-entered. The range to north is of some height, but less than Ábgir. From here the watercourse bends south-west. The Girdánk Nála, from the mountain of that name, comes in on the north.

At about 6¼ miles the kaur turns south. Girdánk hill is visible from here, nearly due north, and apparently only 8 or 9 miles distant.

The broad watercourse bends round to east-south-east, and at 7 miles southwards, into the Ábgir defile. Here the Ábgir Nála joins from west.

The pass, at first about 100 yards wide, winds east for half a mile, and then south-west. Its width is now diminished to 40 yards. Heights on left are 500 or 600 feet and craggy. Road, over cobble stones and small boulders, is tolerable. Good sized pools of rain water are continually met with from the entrance of the defile downwards.*

At 7¾ miles the pass turns east. It is now very narrow, being partially blocked by detached rocks. In places the practicable way is reduced to 10 or 12 yards, and the road for several hundred yards round this corner is decidedly rough. It is, however, perfectly practicable for laden camels. At the end of the rough bit a rainpool, now about 1½ feet deep, is forded. The bottom is good.

At 8 miles bend south-east. The pass now opens to 60 or 70 yards, and its floor is smooth. Here is the kafila halting place known as Ábgir.

A quarter of a mile lower down, the widening defile turns east, and there is a rather long straight reach under the last of the high Ábgir ranges. Towards the end of this the track crosses a bent on the right bank. Road good.

At 9 miles turn west-south-west, bending to west under the further side of the above ridge, and at 9½ miles again south, at which point a few yards are slightly rough. Another track leads under the hill to left to avoid this. The last turn leads through an inferior outer range. Here is the lowest waterhole of Ábgir, and we camped by it, having marched 20½ miles from Harétrak. The baggage mules were nearly 10 hours on the road, which is a trying one for laden animals.

There was plenty of water in the pool, and being soft and sweet rain water, it was highly appreciated by my people. Wood and camel grazing (tamarisk) abundant; also grass.

* Miles' Ábgir was 3 miles from Zorámibeit (Gorám Bént), and must, therefore, have been near the entrance of the gorge, two miles above where we camped.

The kaur here widens at once to 200 yards; but the best, indeed only, camping ground would be on somewhat high bents or gravel plateaux. These are on both sides; the nearest is that to south-east. It is here narrow, but widens to south, and is smooth and level. Road on to it from this side would have to be improved for a few yards.

Goráin Bént is 5 miles from this place.

We passed to-day small camel and donkey kafilas laden with dried fish from Urmára.

It is much warmer here. Minimum of thermometer in the night 42·5.°

This Ábgir water is all from rain. At least the guides say there is no running water, but I believe there is a little. Anyway at this season it is pretty safe to count on a good supply, but it dries up about April. After that the road is rarely travelled. In addition to scarcity of water, the heat is no doubt very great.

The heaviest rain in these parts falls in July and August (*bashám*), and high floods are not uncommon. There is said, however, to be no instance of the road having been closed on account of rain in winter, although a certain amount is expected about now. People hereabouts are Sangúr Balúch, ryats of Mír Kahíra. Their chief is Kammar Khán of Kej. In these hills they muster about 400 men. With them are a few Bizanjaos, the dominant race of south-eastern Mekrán.

Tuesday, 3rd February.—KOHALĆIEN BÉNT. 18¼ miles.

From the last Ábgir waterhole southwards, inclining to east. At 1¾ miles the road under the right bank turns westwards round the corner of a plateau. Scarped clay hills and plateau on the opposite (left) bank of the kaur. (Here we passed a kafila of 12 camels carrying wheat and dried fish from Urmára to Panjgúr). The channel making a sweep to east, the track cuts off the corner, and re-enters it at about 2½ miles. It then turns south to the Wakáb range, under which it turns south-east at 3¼ miles. This is a scarped clayey range about 300 feet high. On the left (north) the kaur is only confined by a high plateau.

At 4 miles turn east, close under the hill, which a quarter of a mile further comes to an end on a plateau, over which there is a track south-east. There are small rain-water holes here.

Wakáb is not a ridge, but a tolerably broad hill. It is continued to the east, but at some distance, by lower, clay hills.

At about 4¾ miles is a rainpool under the scarped bank on the left (north) side of the nála. This is the kafila halting place known as Wakáb. Miles calls it 12 miles from Ábgir; but his halting place was evidently not the same as ours. On the whole I find my estimate of distances agrees closely with his. There is no running stream, although, of course, there may have been one in 1872.

From here the road bends south-east, and lies near the left bank of the kaur.

At about 6 miles there is a low sandhill on the opposite bank. It is called Janika Reg, and near it is a small piece of khushkáwa land. No water.

About here the clay hills begin to assume a flat-topped shape, and lie back from the kaur, which is very wide. Pish has now almost disappeared, and tamarisk is everywhere abundant.

Below Janika Reg the nála is contracted to 250 yards, and the channel further diminished by islands between which the track passes. The road is good.

Thence the nála bends south, and is broad, not less than 400 yards in width. It is joined on the left by the Garání Nála, and at 5 miles bends round to southeast. To south is the Reehók range. A large but shallow rainpool is passed here.

The bends of the kaur are now great sweeps and not short turns. Patches of sandy soil occasionally appear in the bed, and the travelling is altogether easier than heretofore.

At 8 miles turn east under Reehók. The kaur is 100 yards wide, and is bounded on the right (north) by clay hills 50 or 60 feet high, probably the scarp of a plateau.

At 8½ miles bend south-east passing Reehók, which is a narrow range. At 9 miles bend again ; this time south-west. Clay hills on both sides the kaur, which is very broad and pretty thickly grown with tamarisk.

At 9½ miles bend south-south-west. At 10½ miles is Gadag-i-Bént, a low plateau on the left bank. There is perennial running water in the kaur, and the bent is flat, affording ample room for encampment. It is, however, rather stony. On the opposite (west) side of the kaur are small clay hills, and on the east the plateau is bounded by very low ridges. The water here, being slightly saline, is not so good as that of the rainpools. Wood and camel grazing (tamarisk) abundant. Grass, apparently only *drab*, and scanty. Distance to Gorám Bént about 15 miles.

At 13½ miles bend south by west. The road makes a bow line, running parallel to, and near, the right bank of the kaur, which is here the scarp of a plateau. The kaur is a quarter of a mile wide. Low clay hills on the left bank. To south, but at some distance, is the Talóh range, the last of the hills.

At 16 miles the road turn southwards between headlands or islands of plateau, and enters a sort of hollow or narrow valley through which the kaur runs. The water channel is crossed at 17 miles. It is broad and shallow. On either hand are long pools of rain water. Here is the kafila halting place known as Kohalúten Bént, the plateaux on both sides being so called. Thence over soft alluvial soil, rather broken ground, with a good deal of scattered tamarisk and thorn jungle, and low scrub. At 18 miles bend slightly to the right (westwards). The track for some little way lies in a small nála or channel, and is rather heavy.

At 18½ miles the track comes on a pool at least 100 yards long and about a foot deep. Here we camped. Good water and camel grazing abundant. Grass (*barshóa*) moderate. The water is apparently perennial, as it runs a little, is, slightly saline, and is said to last right through the summer.

The hollow is here 300 or 400 yards across, and the plateaux are therefore too far back (as well as too high) to be utilised for encampment. Ground, however, in the neighbourhord of the water could easily be cleared of jungle, and would then be tolerable for camping on. It is partly soft and partly stony.

From here Urmára rock is visible to south and south-east ; also Girdánk, as well as the Abgir and other intervening hills, to the northward.

People hereabouts are mostly Sangúr. The country is evidently a great grazing ground, and there was more than one camp in the immediate neighbourhood. In fact all the way from Kólwáh the country is by no means devoid of inhabitants, and we saw flocks of sheep and goats every day.

It is now warm, but not unpleasantly so. Minimum of thermometer at night 50.°

Wednesday, 4th February.—URMÁRA. 28 miles.

From camp cross the watercourse, and thence wind southwards through broken sandy ground. At 2 miles ascend a low gravel plateau sloping south. This is absolutely the last of the hills. The end of the Talóh range, a mile or more to the west, is now being past, and there is nothing beyond it.

On the plateau the track turns south-west for Urmára. A path to the fishing village of Gazdán leads south. The Síahdád unites with the Súléra Nála between this point and the end of Talóh. The latter watercourse comes from the north-east, and up it lies the road to Chambúr in Kólwáh. From the junction the kaur appears to take the name of Basúl, though the lower Síahdád is also called the Basúl by some.

The stones are soon quitted, and soft broken ground partly covered with tamarisk, &c., is traversed. At 4 miles cross the Basúl Kaur; it is quite dry, and there is heavy sand in the bed. The track leaves it by a narrow and winding side nála.

At 7 miles scattered date trees. Here is the kafila halting place of Basúl. No water on the spot, but some in the kaur a mile or more west. It is a perennial pool. The country is now good level alluvial soil, sprinkled with tamarisk and a few dates, and thickly covered with láni and other small bushes.

At 9 miles the road is fairly out in the open plain, in which is nothing but very low scrub. Some miles to east, where numerous nálas descend from Talóh, is jungle and khushkáwa land. All the country under the hills is good grazing ground, occupied by numerous tumans of Sangúrs and Bízanjaos.*

The Malán hills, beyond which is Hingól, are now plainly visible east-south-east.

The plain gets barer and barer until it is absolutely devoid of vegetation. Here are obvious traces of inundation, and this part is occasionally flooded by hill water.

At 15 miles is a small ridge of rocks on the right hand (south). The road continues parallel to them for about 3 miles. It must not be supposed that because the country is flat and open the route runs straight to its destination. On the contrary it winds about a great deal across between east and south-south-east in a rather irritating manner, as the march is quite long enough without being unnecessarily added to.

At about 21 miles is a patch of verdure in the shape of a small garden watered by wells, one of which is pukka. This place is called Chishé-cháh or Chadé-cláh, or shortly Chad. Inside the gardens are three cutcha wells, one of which is brackish. The pukka well and two or three cutcha ones are outside. Water very good, but not very abundant. Depth of the pukka well about 12 feet.† This and the garden were made by a Mr. Cox of the Telegraph, but now belong to Misri, the chief bannia of Urmára. There was a small cotton field outside the garden.

Ample and good ground for encampment. Camel grazing fair. Grass and wood rather scanty; nearest of the former is *barshóa* in the sand hills to south towards the sea.

From Chad south-east.‡ The track soon enters a long hollow, which looks like, and is, an old lagoon, the entrance to which has silted up. It is quite level and excellent travelling.

At about 4 miles arrive at the beach of Demezar (East Bay), about 2 miles from the village which lies at the extreme end of the isthmus close under the rock. Road good, over tolerably hard sand close to the sea.

The telegraph bungalow is about a mile west of the village on the opposite side of the isthmus. Total distance 28 miles. Road good the whole way. The open country and smoother travelling are a great relief after pursuing a painful way through so many miles of hills.

Thursday, 5th February.—Halted. Visited by the Naib Aladína, son of Álam Khán, Tamarárí Bízanjao, Chief of Urnách, who is governor on behalf of the Jám of Las Bela.

The water-supply of Urmára is from wells or small pits dug in the sand, as at Sunmiání and other places along this coast. It is indifferent. There is one small sweet well near the telegraph bungalow.

No place on the isthmus where troops could be encamped. If there were, the badness of the water and proximity of the ill-smelling village would render a more inland site advisable. Chad, 9 miles (see above), would seem to be the best place for a camp and depôt. The Demezar beach appears well suited for disembarkation, as it is of good firm sand for miles, shelves steadily, and ship's boats could come within 40 yards of the shore at any state of the tide.

Urmára needs no further description than is already on record.

It may be noted, however, that the rock, according to Captain Mockler, is 1,740 feet high.* It has a flat top, which the telegraph employés state is 4 or 5 miles wide in the broadest part. The top of the rock (7 miles long) slopes gradually to the east. The seaward face is somewhat broken, and there is a big ravine on that side, but towards Urmára is a straight unbroken scarp. One very steep and difficult footpath leads to the summit, and there are besides ropes hanging down the cliff in several places, by means of which the inhabitants ascend to get grass. This grows plentifully when there has been any rain. At the present time we got abundance for our horses. It was green and sweet.

Friday, 6th February.—Halted. The Indo-European telegraph has 3 European clerks here, besides native establishment. The bungalow is large, but completely occupied. Was most kindly received and assisted by the telegraph officials. They undertook to see that a coasting craft was sent round for me to Hingól whenever I should require one, and I made arrangements with Basria Mal (Misrí) the leading trader of the place, and farmer of the revenue, for the hire of half a boat whenever I should want it, which I hoped might be in about six weeks.

A register of temperature and rainfall is kept at Urmára. The climate seems very equable. Maximum of thermometer in summer about 85,° seldom rising to 90°.† With a land wind it may be hot for a few days, but not for long. In the cold weather maximum is 72° to 75°. Rain is expected in August—sometimes it falls in July. It is generally a heavy downpour, perhaps several inches at once, and then ceases. The winter rain should be in February, but is only mild showers. Sometimes, however, there is no rain at all, and this may occur for three years in succession. In this case it is probable that the Kólwáh road to Balár, &c., would be impracticable for want of water.

At the end of March and during April high winds occur, and severe dust-storms from the westward.

In May, June, and July damp misty weather brought on by the south-west monsoon.

In November also it is foggy.

December, January, and February are in all respect the best months for moving troops. The weather is settled and pleasant. If there is any rain, it would be an advantage rather than a drawback.

There are six carpenters and three blacksmiths in Urmára. The former are fairly skilful, and build the fishing boats belonging to the port.

Nearly everybody in Urmára speaks Hindustání.

With regard to the duststorms above spoken of, it is alleged that they were unknown 20 years ago. This seems a very remarkable meteorological fact, if true, but it is difficult to believe. The wind is strong enough to shift the sand hills, although the latter are fairly covered with low close growing bushes. It is said that the site of the village has been moved several times on account of unexpected encroachments of sand, and all within the last 15 years.

Of course there is a legend to account for this curse, for so it is not unnaturally deemed by the people. The story goes that about half a generation ago two fakirs visited Urmára, and one of them died there. The then naib seized his goods in spite of the remonstrances of the surviving pilgrim. The latter at once left the place, but before doing so cast a handful of sand towards the village with an anathema, the effect of which is felt in the duststorms of the present day.

It is said that most of the sand blows across the bay from Pasni.

In spite of the legend, it is probable that violent winds, accompanied by clouds of dust, occur at the same season over the whole country as far north as Kandahár. I have experienced them at Kalát, in the Bolán, in Péshín, and in Shoráwak. Several travellers speak of sandstorms in various parts of these regions about the same time of year. They are worth taking notice of, as it is conceivable that they might be a hindrance to military operations.

Maximum of thermometer in the tent ... 82°.
Minimum ... ... 51°.

Pleasant weather; at times slightly cloudy.

From Urmára it was my object to find the shortest and best road into Kólwáh, and from thence to the Gichki valley, with a view to ascertaining the most direct route practicable for troops from Urmára to Khúrán.

After much enquiry it appeared that the only route into Kólwáh, except the one by which we had come, was the road to Chambúr, and we took it accordingly.

Saturday, 6th February.—CHAD. 6 miles. Followed the Padezar beach. It is rather heavy. When about 1½ miles from the conspicuous flat-topped rock called Bírí Kalát, strike north-east across the low sand hills. There is no track here, and the sand for a short distance is somewhat fatiguing to animals, but there is not much of it.

The direct Basúl road used by the telegraph people goes on along the beach to Morpatí lake, and leaving that to the right (east), to Kundekag, 11 miles, which is the first halting place. These are bad wells.

It is much cooler here than under the Urmára rock. Minimum this morning 48°. Heavy dew.

Sunday, 7th February.—CHÍL-A-DAP (BASÚL). 16 miles. Elevation 251 feet.

Went out of the way to visit Kundelag, a cultivated valley between the low range Kánagár, which is that on the west side of Padezar bay, and Gor-la the next ridge inland. Here there are scattered babul trees and date palms, and a good deal of embanked khushkáwa land. Only one well with not much water. There is a watershed between the ranges some distance up. Beyond is more cultivation called Garók. Both inhabited by Sangúr Balúch. No village, only dispersed huts. Altogether they muster about 80 men. Báiáu is chief of Kundelag, and Sháh Dóst of Garók.

The telegraph line, running in a north-westerly direction from the isthmus passes about a mile east of Kundelag (distance 10 miles), and skirts the last rock of Garókí. From about here the Gwádar track (*eid* Pasni ?) divides from the telegraph path, which continues under the wires to Basúl (18 miles).

We left Kundelag by a gap in the ridge (good road), and thence over the plain to the highest water in Basúl Kaur (10½ miles), crossing both the tracks mentioned above at an acute angle.

Camped in bed of nála at a large pool, the nearest to the kafila halting place before mentioned.

The telegraph line crosses about 3 miles lower down, and there is another halting place there also known as Basúl, the latter being an elastic term applied to any spot on or near the kaur.

At telegraph Basúl is a post of the men charged with repairing the line in case of accidents. There is water in pools all the way down from here. A pool above and one below the telegraph line are perennial. No hamlet on the kaur anywhere, only tumans of shepherds. Telegraph Basúl is off the direct route from Kólwáh, but it shortens the long march into Urmára.

Kundelag would be a good place for a first march from Urmára *if the water supply were improved*, and there is little doubt this might be done. Water would appear to exist in the valley at a depth of 12 to 15 feet. Local labour would suffice to sink 8 or 10 wells in 10 days or so, and there is every probability of the supply proving sufficient for a considerable body of troops. If detained for several days, their transport might go on to telegraph Basúl, where there is plenty of water, grass, and camel forage. Both Chad and Kundelag might be used as first halting places for troops bound northwards; and they had better be marched there immediately on landing. Officers should, however, be sent previously to prepare the ground and water-supply.

Morpatí lake, passed on the road from Urmára to Kundelag, soon after leaving the beach, is a hollow filled by rain from the hills. There is almost always water in it throughout the winter, but it happens to be dry this season. It remains sweet for about three months after first filling, but gets brackish as it dries up, and when low the water is quite undrinkable.

The proper name of the place where we are now is Tekás, or Chíl-a-Daf, the latter being apparently the best known. The pool is perennial; that is to say, it is not mere rain water, but lasts through the hot weather in ordinary times. Of course after 3 or 4 years drought this, and every other drop of water in the country, is likely to be dried up. The water of the Basúl Kaur is considered excellent.[*] The channel is here a quarter of a mile wide; banks alternately scarped and shelving; bed sandy. Jungle of large tamarisks extends half a mile on either side of the nála. This affords abundant wood and camel grazing. Grass is also plentiful; it is coarse *drab*, but is found green in the side nálas.

The best camping ground would be on the left bank above the water. Descent to the latter easy.

---

[*] The pools, however, are very muddy, and the water requires clearing with alum to be palatable to Europeans.

Monday, 8th February.—RÚNGÁN-A-DAF. 13 miles. Elevation 398 feet.

This march is to the mouth of a small nála above Gadag-i-Bént, where the Chambúr road branches from that to Balúr.

The track ascends the left bank of the kaur till the kafíla route is struck, and it then follows the latter, passing Kohalúien Bent at about 5 miles (*vide* diary of 3rd February).

There is, however, a more direct track, which follows the Súléra Nála. By this it is 20 miles from Chíl-a-Daf to Gazí, and there is no intermediate water. Moreover the Súléra and Takár Kands, crossed on this route, are said to be difficult, though lightly laden camels can get over them.* We took the longer road, as it appears the most suitable for troops.

The nála opposite to the mouth of which we are camped is Rúngán. It is distinguished as Kuléri. Rúngán Kuléri is the name of a green prickly bush common in Sind as well as here.

Minimum of thermometer this night 61°. To-day and yesterday very hot, and nights oppressive.

Troops would not camp here, but at Gadag-i-Bént just below.

Tuesday, 9th February.—CHETRAO (MASID). 17 miles. Elevation 1,089 feet.

Eastwards up the nála, which is broader than it looks from the outside. Average width 80 or 90 yards. Ascent very easy, just perceptible, and road good. Clay hills on either hand. These are scarped as usual, and some are several hundred feet high.

I call these hills, clay hills, because they look like clay at a little distance, and it is a convenient term. As a matter of fact, they are mostly composed of slaty shale, only differing from that of the high ranges to the north in being more decomposed. The original rock is in many places so disintegrated near the surface that it crumbles between the fingers. The surface of the hills is covered with a whitish earthy film exceedingly soft and loose. A few inches down, however, the rock is still pretty firm, and at the depth of a foot, where not exposed to the weather, it is as hard as brick. All these ranges are exceedingly weather worn. The action of the elements has cut and carved them into strange peaks and ridges, and every slope is deeply grooved. At least one side of every hill is scarped, often sheer down from the summit. The slaty shales are banded with metamorphic claystone (at least I call it so for want of a better name). It appears of all thicknesses, but generally 6" to 18." The dip of the strata being always considerable, sheets of this claystone are often exposed to the air, and then present a curious corrugated appearance. The cleavage being at right angles, it splits into rectangular fragments, not unlike bricks; and where these are numerous, they make the ground rough travelling.

The clay ridges preserve the parallelism in common to all the ranges of the country, but this is only observable when at some little height above them; otherwise they appear a tumbled mass of small peaks with interlaced spurs. When flat topped, it will be found that the shales are invariably overlaid by a layer of conglomerate. There is little or no vegetation on these hills, but the large watercourses have a scanty growth of tamarisk, thorny shrubs, and pish.

The clay hills are not peculiar to southern Mekrán. They are found in many parts of Baluchistán. I do not know whether they are connected with the "Gáj beds" of Blandford and Griesbach.

---

* These kands are on a clay hill range. They are not high, and the difficulty appears to consist in the steepness of the road.

The outer ranges from Talóh southwards are of sandstone, and appear lithologically similar to those at the mouth of the Nárí, &c., which are classified under the head of the "Mánchar" series.

For about six miles the nála is tolerably straight. It then winds a good deal, with a northward inclination for 1¾ miles, and is narrower. Road good. At about 7¼ miles it suddenly becomes only a few yards wide, and in less than 100 yards reaches a small kotal between high clay peaks. This is called the Kulérí Kand. According to the aneroid it is 660 feet higher than the bed of the Síahdád (Basúl), where the latter is quitted.

Descent from thence is considerably greater than the ascent. For the first few yards it is about 1 in 4. This leads to a rather narrow and deep winding ravine, which is followed for about 3 miles.

At 10¾ miles enter the Chetrao Kaur, a large watercourse running from east to north-west. It joins the Síahdád (Basúl) between Wakáb and the Reehók hills. I think its debouchure must be what was pointed out to me as the Garání. The latter is said to be comparatively small.

Follow the Chetrao eastwards. It is at least 200 yards wide, and closely resembles the Síahdád, except that its course is here straighter. Road over the stones not so good. Some small rainpools are passed here. At about 13½ miles climb the left bank on to an elevated bent; bare and stony, but flat. It is called Tojí. Road good.

At 14½ miles descend again to the kaur. Here the direct road viâ Gazí joins in, having come through the hills on the right (south). Path continues eastwards up the kaur to the camping place. Here there is a small pool of rain water under a high cliff on the left hand (north). The best camping ground would seem to be just short of this on an elevated plateau on the same side.

The whole of this march lies between clay ranges, but parallel to them on the north are considerable hills called Máhpál, and the nála turns towards them at this point.

Water here is uncertain. Wood and camel grazing (tamarisk) abundant; also coarse grass (*drab*).

The spot is best known by the name of Masid (Masjid) from a praying place at some little distance.

This is Umarárí Bízanjao country. The Sangúrs are now left to west. The Umarárís are the section residing about Chambúr.

Cloudy all day, and a smart shower at 5-30 P.M. Very warm.

Wednesday, 10th February.—GANDAGAR. 11 miles. Elevation 1,806 feet.

North-north-east from the water. Road good, alongside scarp on the left. The nála sweeps round to north, and at about two miles is crossed. Here is a waterhole under the wall on the left hand.

The track is now rough for a few yards, and then re-enters the nála bed, where it is fair going. Direction north. At 3 miles enter the defile known as Chetrao Dát through the Máhpal hill. It is at first 80 or 90 yards wide. The heights on either hand are high and steep. They are mostly composed of stratified claystone overlying slaty shales.

The defile soon narrows to 30 yards, and in some places less. It winds among spurs, but the road is good. There is a little running water here.

At 3¾ miles the pass widens, having traversed the high range. Here the Karpad Nála comes in from the left (west), and joins the Gandagar from right (east) to form the Chetrao.

Track (following Gandagar) now bends north-east round a small projecting plateau. Then east, back under the high dark Máhpál range. On the left (north) are clay hills, and beyond them a considerable light colored range called the Ríshk-i-Band. It is visible from Koháluien Bént, &c., and thence appears to be one with Máhpal.

The watercourse is here 40 to 50 yards wide. Road good. There is water everywhere from the entrance of the defile. Most of it is no doubt due to yesterday evening's shower, but there seems to be a small running stream as well.

At about five miles three furlongs the nála is rather contracted, with a high plateau on left. At 6 miles it turns north-east, and winds through the clay hills for nearly a mile towards the base of Rishk-i-Band, which for the first time becomes conspicuous.

The track now passes through a sort of narrow gully for a short distance, cutting off a bend of the nála.

The latter is now much wider, and while heretofore nearly bare, it is now grown with tamarisk, pish, and grass.

At $9\frac{1}{2}$ miles turn sharp to left (north) towards Ríshk. The parallel ranges continue to run eastwards for a long distance. The space between them, about a mile or a mile and a half wide is filled up with clay hills and plateaux. Through these comes the Pardén Nála and joins Gandagar at the bend.

At about 10 miles enter defile in the Ríshk-i-Band. It is at first about 20 yards wide, but very soon it is narrowed by rocks, till there is just room for one animal to pass. At the same time the way lies through a pool, now about a foot deep, but probably often dry. Beyond, the path is rough for a few yards. This is rather an awkward bit for laden animals, but it is very short.

Thence east-north-east, defile 20 yards wide as before. The bottom is smooth and road good. After some little way again turn north and wind between spurs for a quarter of a mile or so. Here are more rocks and water, but there is no difficulty. Exit is into a broken valley or upland country of clay hills.

This would be an easy pass to defend. The heights are hardly accessible from the south. Of course the country is perfectly friendly.

Camped just outside on right bank of nála. Water from within the defile.

No good camping ground. Fuel (pish) abundant, but camel grazing scanty. Grass (*gurkao*) abundant on the hills.

Much cooler to-day, owing no doubt to the rapid increase of elevation. According to the aneroid, the rise has been over 100 feet a mile ever since entering the Chetrao, and 1,400 feet in eleven miles from last camp. One would not imagine it to be nearly so much.

Thursday, 11th February.—(Sordrígí). 23 miles. Elevation 2,255 feet.

Road follows the nála in a general north-easterly direction. After a mile there are rather high hills on the right hand. Low clay elevations on left. The road, over bents, is very good.

At $1\frac{1}{2}$ miles again north-east, and then east through the same insignificant parallel ranges. The clay hills, however, give place to clay slate, and the change is apparent in the goodness of the road.

At about 3 miles turn north for a short distance, and then east. At $3\frac{3}{4}$ miles leave the Gandagar Nála, last seen coming from the east, and wind northwards through small rocky hills.

Here are several tracks. Laden camels take the longest, but the most direct is easy enough. It crosses a very low kotal, and descends into a ravine, where it is joined by the other at 4¼ or 4½ miles. The ravine is contracted immediately below, and there is a rough descent of a few yards through a rocky little defile or gap, after which the road is again easy, and there is a gentle descent northwards down the watercourse.

This leads at about 4¾ miles to a rather large nála running from east to west, and called the Píru. Here there are two roads; the longest and easiest turns up the nála. The other crosses it, and winds north and north-east up a ravine through low rocky hills. At one place the way is only sufficient to allow a camel to pass, but the track is smooth.

At 5 miles reach the summit of a kotal called Píru-a-Kand. From hence there is a limited view northwards over a monotonous succession of low brown ranges, beyond which is the somewhat higher ridge called Kalát-Koh-i-Band.

The descent from the Pass is by a zigzag path for about 200 yards; it is a little rough, but quite practicable for any laden animal. Thence bend round to east up a ravine, road easy, and cross a small kotal or neck, from which is another steep but short descent to a ravine leading north. Here the camel route joins in.

Troops would probably take the direct path over the kand, leaving the other for the baggage.

At 6 miles enter the Shír Kumb, a good sized kaur, thickly grown with drab grass and pish. The track turns up it and leads north-eastward between low parallel ranges as usual. The road is sometimes in the nála and sometimes over bents, but always excellent.

At 9¼ miles cross a watershed. Elevation (by aneroid) about 1,956 feet. Eastward the drainage is to the Hingól river, and westward to the Basúl. The broken valley or hollow is seen extending north-east from the watershed for a long distance.

The track, however, turns east, and after about half a mile enters the hills; but as soon as the first ridge is passed, it again turns north-east.

At about 10¼ miles a low neck is crossed, and the road continues north-east down a small ravine between low hills as usual.

At about 10¾ miles turn north through another ridge. Thence in a general north-easterly direction down a shallow pish grown nála through a sort of half open country.

At 12¼ miles ascend the left bank of the kaur to a somewhat elevated gravel plain of considerable extent. The country is now open both east and west for a long distance. Road north-east and very good.

At 13¼ miles traverse low hills diagonally, and cross another gravel plateau north north-east.

At 14½ miles descend into a nála with high banks plentifully grown with pish and tamarisk. This is the Párkíní Kaur. It seems to be the principal drainage channel of this part of the hills, and runs east to the Hingól river. It is crossed, but much lower down, by the Gúrad road from Urmára (see Routes), and is said there to contain running water.

The track turns up the kaur, ascending the left bank at 15 miles, but soon descending again. At about 15¼ miles the right bank is climbed. It is high and rather steep. An elevated gravel plateau is now crossed, and the kaur entered for the third time at 16¼ miles.

The road leads across it, but a short distance up, under a rock on the left hand side, is a good sized rainpool. A plateau on the opposite (right) bank would probably be found the best camping ground. Water of course somewhat uncertain, but some is pretty sure to be found hereabouts in an average season.* Very often there is a pool or two lower down near where the road first strikes the kaur; and if so it would be a better place at which to halt. Wood, camel grazing, and grass abundant. This spot is called Dádigor. Road good all the way.

From the upper pool return a short distance down the kaur to where the road last enters. The track crosses the nála and leads in a general north-east direction up an affluent watercourse on the opposite side. It is 40 or 50 yards wide, and closed by low hills on both sides. The road is good.

At 3 miles turn east; the Kalát Kóh range is now near on the left. At 3½ miles turn north to the foot of the hills, whence ascend by a good winding path to a low kotal called the Resh Kand. The descent is also easy down a ravine, which leads into a larger watercourse coming from the east. This is descended, and almost immediately joins the Párkiní Kaur (4 miles).

The Párkiní goes away to the westward between the ranges, and then bends round to Dádigor.

Thence north-east ascending the kaur, here shallow, but still a considerable watercourse, thickly grown with písh. Low hills on both sides. Road good.

At about 5 miles there are two tracks—that to right follows the nála east-north-east, and being the easiest is that usually followed by laden camels. The other bends away north-west up a small clay slate watercourse through comparatively open ground for a quarter of a mile or more. It then descends into a nála running south to the Párkiní Kaur, and turning up it, north, enters the hills almost immediately. Here is a short gap or gorge called Ábgir, the further end of which is narrowed to 5 yards, and the practicable way lies through a pit or waterhole only 3 feet wide. Animals have to plunge down into this and climb out again, and if full of water, it would be an awkward bit. It is, however, turned by the path mentioned above, which is quite easy.

From here the track ascends to a low plateau with the watercourse on the right.† The latter is soon re-entered (here camel road comes in), and followed in a general northerly direction through broken ridges and detached hills of inconsiderable elevation. Road good.

At about 6¼ miles turn west, and almost immediately come on surface water. The nála bed is covered with saline incrustations, but the water is pure and sweet.

This is Sordrúgí, and we camped. Water abundant and good. Fuel plentiful. Camel grazing moderate. *Gurkoo* grass abundant on the hills.

There is, however, no place to camp, and being so near Párkiní Kaur, troops would generally go straight thence to Chambúr.

Baggage mules were to-day 9¾ hours doing the march. It is on the whole a wonderfully good road, but both men and animals are footsore, and weary of the eternal hills.

People here, and in fact along the whole route, are Umarárí Bizanjaos under Mandao Khán of Chambúr.

Cool weather. Minimum of thermometer 40°.

---

* It is said to last right through the summer.
† There is water here and room to camp, but the former is rather brackish.

One of the ponies died this night. We have nine transport mules and three ponies. They are all lightly laden; but whereas the mules have hitherto done their work steadily and satisfactorily, the ponies have often carried no loads at all, and are nevertheless completely exhausted. A second is in a hopeless condition. Grass has been pretty plentiful everywhere, but I think the grain ration (4 lbs) is not enough for ponies. They seem to want more than mules.

Friday, 12th February.—CHAMBÚR. 10½ miles. Elevation 2,144 feet.*

West for a little way up the watercourse; then follow it north through a ridge; then again west inclining to north-west. Lowhills as usual. Road good.

Still following the nála turn north, and at one mile enter a small defile between hills of some height. It is about 70 yards long and only 3 or 4 wide. Road fair.

Thence north-north-east, and after a quarter of a mile the nála, passing through small hills, is again contracted.

After this turn west-north-west through a fairly open valley or hollow. A range several hundred feet high is on the right. This is gradually approached, and the road crosses it at 2 miles by a low easy kotal. This is the watershed of Kólwáh. To south the drainage is to the sea by the Hingól river. Kólwáh proper is a basin with no drainage outlet.

From the kand, north-north-west through a broken valley full of small hills. It drains west and north to the Kólwáh plain.

At about 3 miles descend to a nála called Shándí, and follow it down, winding through the hills. At 3¾ miles leave this (which goes west) and cross a bent, descending into a small watercourse.

This is also soon quitted (it goes west to the Shándí), and the road passes over another plateau.

At about 4¼ miles it rounds the end of a spur, and turns north-east for Chambúr, the fort of which, on a high light colored isolated rock, is now visible.

The remainder of the road leads over gravelly *dámán*, passing the ends of several small ranges on the right. The watercourses, so shallow as to be hardly distinguishable as such, are fairly well wooded with small babul, tamarisk, and shrubs. Alluvial soil is not struck till within a mile and a half of the fort. It is banked khushkáwa land, and the track as usual winds along the bunds.

Before reaching this, however, at about 8½ miles the main road running through Kólwáh from Kej to Áwárán and Gwarjak is crossed.

Camped at foot of rock on south-west side.

Violent westerly wind to-day with clouds of dust. The haziness always produced by a high wind made surveying difficult.

A post in to-day. Jacobabad letters up to 9th January. None of mine received up to that date.

Saturday, 13th February.—Halted. Surveying. Most unfortunately a furious wind and dust made work almost impossible.

The cultivation around here is not very extensive. This year there are only a few fields to the south-west. The plain in the immediate neighbourhood is covered with láni and scattered jungle of low trees. A mile and a half west, however, is the edge of the great bare expanse, which occupies nearly the whole

---

* This place would appear to be more than 100 feet lower than Surdrúgi. The high wind depressing the barometer has not improbably given it a fictitious elevation. In fact none of the elevations are trustworthy. The barometer made Balúr 944 feet and Chambúr 2,144 feet; a difference of exactly 1,200 feet. Judging however by the lie of the country they are of nearly the same elevation. Chambúr being probably the lowest!

of this portion of Kólwáh. It is absolutely naked, without even the smallest shrub or tuft of vegetation, and bears very evident traces of flooding. It was explained to us that this tract is a lake when any considerable amount of rain falls, as the drainage of all the surrounding hills is here collected and cannot escape. It is said that the water occasionally reaches a depth of several feet.* No attempt is made to cultivate this plain, the soil, it is said, being too salt.

On the opposite side of the valley to Chambúr, and about 4 miles north therefrom, is Hor, a Naoshírwání village. At harvest time as many as 100 families are collected here. There is a fort on a mound, containing a well, and there is another well outside. The land is khushkáwa. The chief of Hor is Balúch Khán (a nephew of Ázád Khán), the same whose depredations have driven the Kaodáis from all their Kólwáh lands except Nág. He has himself however, been sufficiently intimidated by the Bízanjaos to retire to Khárán with the view of obtaining assistance from Ázád Khán.

Also on the opposite side of the valley, about 8 miles west of Hor, and 10 miles west-north-west of Chambúr, is Mádag. Here is a good deal of khushkáwa land, and the village formerly consisted of 100 houses; but there are very few people living there now, as the inhabitants have fled to Gwarkóp to escape from Balúch Khán. There are three wells at Mádag, and plenty of water for drinking purposes.

The Mádag Kand, described as a high pass,† lies several miles north-east of the village, and is approached by a ravine. In general characteristics it probably resembles the Hodál Kand, and is on the same range, but it is said to be decidedly more difficult. The road joins the Urmára—Panjgúr road just above the Gúmbak halting place as already noted.

Between Mádag and Hor is a spring near the edge of the dámán with a few date trees. It is called Sháhí, and belongs to Balúch Khán of Hor.

Chambúr is a fort on an isolated rock some 80 or 90 feet high. The rock is steep (but not inaccessible) on the west, and the fort, in three tiers, crowns the summit, and extends down the east side. It is considered large and strong for this part of the world, and would probably hold 200 or 250 men, but might be defended by 50.

All the walls are high enough to give good cover, and are well loopholed. The material is rough stone mortared with mud. There is a well in the outer enclosure, nearly 100 feet deep, and containing abundance of good water. This is the only well in Chambúr. The fort would no doubt give trouble, even to regular troops, if unprovided with artillery; but the new mountain gun would probably breech the walls, and the place seems rather a shell trap. It is commanded by a low ridge on the south, half a mile distant, and rocks on the east afford cover at much less. The surrounding soil is easily worked, and is now banked in some places for cultivation.

Mandao Khán, Chief of the Umarárí Bízanjáos, resides with his family in the fort.‡ Round about the base of the rock are clustered about 40 huts of the tribe, but not many people live here in winter.

---

* In 1876 the highest flood known reached to the base of the low hills south of Chambúr Fort. There the water was knee deep, and in the plain 6 feet. The season for floods is in July and August, but they do not by any means occur every year.

† There are said to be *seven* kotals. From Mádag the first march would be to Kajhma Ravi, about 16 or 17 miles. This is a nála which joins the Kil Kaur above where the Panjgúr road crosses. Kajhma is a march from Gúmbak, where the Mádag road joins that from Balár.

‡ He is not here now, having gone to Awárán with some men to punish the Mirwárís of Beh for plundering certain Umárárís. His son Yár Muhammad did the honours. He is a man of about 30, and struck me as being intelligent, though reserved. It may be remarked here that a large number of the people in these parts are by religion "Zikurs," and not Muslims. Yár Muhammad is noted as being *neither*.

There is plenty of room to camp, but the existence of only a single source of water-supply, and that in the fort, would be inconvenient to a body of troops of any size. Grass is scanty and brought from a long distance. Wood and camel grazing abundant.*

Not many camels are bred in Kólwáh, but there are many bullocks, and abundance of sheep and goats. These are mostly grazed in the hills to south. For some reason wheat does not succeed here. Barley only is grown, and barley meal is universally eaten. As there are no streams, there are no water mills.

It is well to make a few notes regarding the state of affairs in Kólwáh. Ever since reaching Khózdár we have been hearing a good deal about the disturbances in this district. Kólwáh is, in fact, always more or less disturbed, but just now the situation is rather more serious than usual.

The present difficulty seems to have arisen out of the old affair between the Kaodais and the Naoshírwánís of Ilor. The Naoshírwánís who first settled in Kólwáh were few,† and lived very much on sufferance. As they became more numerous, and were certain of support from Khárán, they grew bolder; but it was not until the present Balúch Khán, now a man of about 60, became chief, that their neighbours seem to have had cause for complaint.

Balúch Khán, however, is said to have systematically oppressed and plundered all weaker than himself. The Kaodais in particular, being peaceable and not very warlike, have suffered greatly at his hands, and last spring deserted Sigak, Rodakán, and Balúr—in fact, almost all their lands in Kólwáh—and went off to their fellow tribesmen in Gwarkóp.

I do not know what amount of resistance, if any, the Kaodais opposed to the exactions of the Naoshírwánís, but it is said they paid tribute to Balúch Khán's father and grandfather. Abdul Karím, Mírwárí, Chief of Bédí, and Naib of Kolwáh and Mashkai, not only afforded no protection to the Kaodai, but desired to levy tribute on them himself. Whether he did this for his own advantage, or only in the way of collecting revenue for the Khán, is uncertain. It is, however, apparent that being connected by marriage with Ázád Khán, and in close alliance with the Naoshírwánís, he has encouraged rather than checked Balúch Khán in his evil practices.

Last year, Fakír Khán, a small Bízanjao chief of Jao, married a daughter of the principal Kaodai Sirdar, and informed Balúch Khán and Abdúl Karím that they need not expect to get anything more out of the Kaoduis, as they were now under Bízanjáo protection, and whatever they paid would be taken in future by himself and Mír Kahírí. Thereupon fighting began. The Bízanjao made common cause with Fakír Khán and the Káodais against the Mírwárís and Naoshírwánís, and an engagement took place at Rodakán, in which the former lost six men and the latter four; but the Bízanjaos seem on the whole to have got the best of it, and obtained some plunder from the Naoshírwánís. Here matters might possibly have rested had not a near relative of Mír Kahírí Hasil Khán, died of a wound received in the skirmish. The Bízanjaos then declared they would continue the contest, and being too strong for their opponents, both Balúch Khán and Abdul Karím have gone to Khárán to get assistance from thence.

---

* With regard to the water-supply, there are wells on the dámán of the hills to south, but at some little distance. These are the Múrghi Cháh, Kúrki Cháh, and two others. There is some water in the Múrghi Kaur, and it is said to be utilised for cultivation. The Shándí Nála also contains a little water, at least at times.

† See also Sir Charles Macgregor's "Wanderings in Blúchistán."

Such, omitting details, is the state of affairs, so far as they can be made out from various confused and contradictory accounts. There has been no fighting since the affair in Rodakán about six months ago. The assembled Bízanjaos after that marched to Áwárán—almost within musket shot of Bédí—but the Mírwárís were apparently not strong enough to venture out of their walls, and after some time the Bízanjaos dispersed. It is expected, however, that as soon as Azád Khán's men come down there will be a more or less serious engagement.

The Khán's part in all this has been to summon Abdul Karím and Mír Kahírá to Kalát, but both have declined to obey the order. I believe he also sent the latter a small detachment of troops, and we heard once that they were engaged in besieging the fort at Sámí.

Once before Azád Khán sent a force into Kólwáh. This was some seven years ago*, and at that time Balúch Khán was in alliance with the Bízanjaos. The force was sent to assist his rival Lála, also a Naoshírwání, and it amounted, it is said, to 1,500 well armed men. The Bízanjaos, thinking this body too strong for them, retired into the hills, and there does not seem to have been any fighting.

Sunday, 14th February.—MÁLÁR (*riá* ZÍK). 17½ miles. Elevation 2,241 feet.

North-north-east over the plain to low hills called Sokálí Par. The soil is good, but has evidently not been cultivated for some time. Kulér, tamarisk, and bér trees are thickly sprinkled, and a low scrub of láni covers the ground.

At about 1½ miles reach the hills and pass through them. Some cultivation here.

Thence the road turns north-east by east parallel to the hills, but at about 5¼ miles divides, the track to Zík branching to the left, while that to Málár is straight on.

Through jungle as before. The ruinous fort of Zík is reached at 8½ miles. It is well situated on a large mound, probably artificial. The builder was Fakír Muhammad, Mírwárí (but to be confused with the Bízanjao naib of the same name). We heard a confused story of Fakír Muhammad having fought, like every body else, with Balúch Khán of Hor, and thereafter having gone on a pilgrimage to Mecca, where he died. At any rate the fort has been abandoned for about 8 years (since 1876). This Fakír Muhammad was a cousin of the present Naib, Abdul Karím.

There is a well in the fort, now choked, but it could easily be cleared. Another well is at the base of the mound on the west side. It is about 50 feet deep, and contains abundance of good water. Camels, sheep, and goats were being watered at it as we passed.

There is some khushkáwa cultivation about Zík belonging to Mírwárís.

A good camping ground could easily be found. Wood, water, and camel grazing abundant ; but no grass fit for horses within some miles. The nearest is beyond low hills to the north-west.

Met some Muhammad Hasání shepherds here. This is the furthest southward limit of that tribe.

From Zík through jungle as before, east-north-east towards the low hills. At 1 mile from the fort is a well said to contain plenty of water.

The road keeps along the *dámán* of the low hills (called Tobai), and at about 5¾ or 6 miles crosses a watershed, the exact spot being not easily distinguishable.

---

* 1874.

Thence over alluvial soil, with cultivation in several places. Small trees of kulér, &c., are abundant.

At 17½ miles reach the first of the two Málár villages. We camped on the east side.

Kólwáh, which from the Panjgúr road eastward to Chambúr is an open plain 8 to 10 miles across, is here divided longitudinally by a long range of low hills. About Chambúr the plain, previously lying west and east, bends up north-east, but the curve is sufficiently gradual to be imperceptible to the eye. The dividing ridge, like the other hills, lies north-east and south-west. To its south-east are Marao—a flood basin (the word "marao" means a tract liable to inundation), the Rek-i-Cháh halting place, and, to north-east of the latter, Gúshanah. To north-west of the ridge is Zík, and to its north-east the Málár villages.

Fortunately very little wind to-day, but it began to blow suddenly about sun-down, and blew hard all night. The wind is from the north, and is chilly. It is evident that the windy season has set in earlier than usual, and there is every reason to fear great hindrance to work.

Monday, 15th February.—Halted. Surveying. It would have been useless trying to march to-day in a raging duststorm. The wind went down about noon, but began again at sunset.

The chief of this place is Músa Khán, a cousin of Abdul Karím. He informs me he once went from hence to Khárán. First to the Gitehkí Kaur, in two days, halting midway at Doráskí. Thence, by Sákán Kalát and the Múrgáp Pass, to Nágha Kalát on the third day; from Nágha to Páhliáz on the fourth day; and thence to Khárán in 2 or 3 days.* He is the first person I have been able to find who has been to Khárán by a direct south road, and his route is very much what I should have laid down from information received at various places. He confirms details already learned regarding the Páhliáz road, and it now only remains to personally explore the road from here into Gitchk, when we shall know as much about the routes from Urmára to Khárán as is possible without going right into forbidden territory.

Málár consists of two villages—Músa Khán's, at which we are camped, and another about a mile north-east. The maliks of the latter are Dostén, Músa's sister's son, and Dost Muhammad, stepfather of the latter. Both are poor looking collections of pish and mat huts, each having now about 120 of these hovels. Músa's fort is, however, much better than Dost Muhammad's, but that is not saying much. It is a small irregular structure badly built of rude mud bricks. The walls are about 12 feet high and loopholed. There are several towers. Inside is a well, 70 or 80 feet deep, containing an abundant supply of good water. Another well is without to the east; it has but little water, and that indifferent. At Dost Muhammad's village are also two wells, one within and one without the fort. There is a very fair amount of cultivation in the neighbourhood of the villages. The crops looked well for khushkáwa, and more forward than at Chambúr. The fighting strength of the Mirwárís is said to be altogether 1,000 men. In Kolwáh 400. The chief, Abdul Karím, is also entitled to the support of the cognate clans Kalandaráni, Rodéní, Gúrganárí, and Sumalárí. The two former inhabit Gidar, and are supposed to muster about 500 and 300 men respectively. The Gúrganárís are found in

---

* Each of these stages is a good day's ride; for instance, from Mákúr to Doraski is 32 miles. The route is almost entirely through hills, except the last part, which is sand desert. "Doraski" is of course some place on the kaur of that name, probably Zawardam Laf. See Routes XI C., and XI A.

Júl and Lakorián, and can turn out about 700 men. The Sumaláris have Kolak and Korás, and are also found in Greshak and Nál. The chief of the latter lives at Gidar, as before mentioned. These Sumaláris must be quite distinct from the Mingal branch of the same name, but it is extraordinary how difficult it is to come to an understanding about any Bráhúí tribe. In these parts the Sumalárí Mingals have never been heard of. All the above are supposed to furnish a contingent to Abdul Karím in time of war, but they have declined to join in the present contest with the Bízanjaos. The Kambaránís are not directly connected with the Mírwárís.*

Gúshanah is another Mírwárí village, 6 or 7 miles to the south-east. It consists of a fort on a rock like that of Chambúr, and of, at most, 100 huts. The chief is Walí Mahammad. There are also a few Mírwárís about Reg-i-Cháh, said to be 8 miles south of Málár. This place is a well in Marao. The latter is described as an oval plain, or basin, receiving the drainage of Zík, Málár, Gúshanah, &c., and of course of the hills to north and south of those places. It differs from the basin west of Chambúr in not being dák or clear plain, but is, on the contrary, covered with grass jungle, which, when there has been much rain, reaches a height of 6 feet or more. It does not seem to become deeply flooded like the other plain. There is no marsh as the name would seem to imply. It is also smaller, apparently long and narrow. The grass is good. When dry the old stuff is burnt off.

Plenty of ground to camp might be found about Málár, and water from the two villages would probably be sufficient for a considerable force. Wood and camel grazing abundant, but grass is scanty and brought from a distance.

In the event of a force marching from Urmára to Khárán, by this route, either Chambúr or Málár would have to be made a depôt. Latter for choice, Marao *might* furnish grass; otherwise gangs of men and local carriage would have to be employed to bring it in from the hills.

Wind dropped to-day for a short time about noon, but soon recommenced. The night was very cold.

Tuesday, 16th February.—TÁLÁR. 19 miles. Elevation 3,990 feet.

The Whálí road to Gítehk strikes about north-north-east from Málár, ascending the *dámán* of the hills to where the Whálí Kaur leaves the range called Hazár-guzí, or the hills of a thousand ibex. It is a good road, and descends into the nala at about 9 miles from Málár.

I went past the second village, about half way (4 miles) to Bázdár. Here there is a watershed from which both Málár and Bázdár are visible. To southwest the drainage is to Marao; to north-east the water flows to the Hingól river. We then turned north for the Whálí defile. No road, and the dámán rather rough. At about 2 miles crossed a track leading to Gwarjak, &c. It is shorter than the roads up the valley, but indifferent. Joined the road where the latter descends into the nala, and turns up it into the hills.

The pass is only 40 or 50 yards wide, enclosed between high clay slate hills. The road is generally very good, and the gorge rather picturesque. After some miles, the first high ranges having been passed, the hills become lower.

The track is well marked, but several ravines join the Whálí, looking as large as itself. Up one of these, called Jaki, there is water, and tracks lead into it. The right hand road is the proper one.

* The communication these parts is that there were three brothers—Ahmad, Kambar, and M........ ... in the Ahmadzais (ruling family), the Kambaranís, and the Mírwárís are respectively descended. N......... ...... tract.

At about 5 miles from the entrance (14 from Málár) three nálas meet, the most easterly being a trifle below the others. We discovered by the tracks that our baggage had gone into this, and were obliged to follow it, although the centre watercourse is the right road.

After some 5 miles of galloping up a narrow but smooth ravine, leading eastward behind the ranges, we came on the baggage. It was then half an hour after sunset, and everything had been unloaded. So we perforce remained for the night.

Water here from holes in the bed of the watercourse. No room even for our small party to camp. We had to settle down as best we could. Grass abundant. Wood and camel grazing sufficient.

There is no road whatever up this ravine. It becomes impassable, except for footmen, a short distance higher up. The word Tálár, which frequently occurs in this country, appears to mean *inaccessible*.

Bitterly cold wind all day.

Wednesday, 17th February.—DUZÁNGARO.14½ miles. Elevation 3,441 feet.

Descended the Tálár ravine for 5 miles to regain the proper road. This leads up the main nála, only divided from Tálár by a spur. On the left hand is an elevated plateau.

At 1¼ miles from the point where the road is regained (15¼ from Málár) the Whálí is quitted, and the track leads up a ravine in an east-north-easterly direction. This ravine is only separated from Tálár by a single narrow range. It is at first about 25 yards wide, but gradually narrows. The road is good.

A track up the Whálí is said eventually to join the Balúr—Panjgúr road at Zám. There is no road into the Doráski Kaur.

Some 2 miles up the ravine (17 or 17½ miles from Málár) is surface water. According to the guide it is called Whálí, though that kaur has been altogether quitted. At all events it is the first water on the road. There is no room to camp, and hardly even to bivouac. Half a mile up, however, is more water, and here troops might manage to spend the night on spurs to the left (north). Grass is tolerably abundant on the hills. Wood and camel grazing very moderate. From about the first water the rise becomes very perceptible, and the ranges on either hand are high and close.

About 1½ miles further there is more water. From hence the ascent is rapid In another half mile the ravine becomes very narrow, and the road, hitherto very good, is slightly rough for a few yards. A short distance beyond this, about 20 miles from Málár and 2 from the second water, the watershed of the ravine is reached. It is very narrow, and sunk between spurs of the clay slate ranges.

This is called the Duzángaro Kand,* and Duzáugaro is also applied to the ravines on both sides.

Last night's halting place is only just on the far side of the southern ridge, probably not more than a rifle shot off, after more than 11 miles of marching.

The descent is down a narrow ravine, and is very steep for the first few yards. After winding for about half a mile water is reached, and here is the usual halting place called Duzángaro. It would, however, be very inconvenient for troops, as there is no room anywhere. Thence follow watercourse winding in a general north-easterly direction. The average width of the ravine is 20 to 30 yards, but it is narrowed by rocks in several places. The road is good all along, and water appears at short distances.

---

* Elevation about 4,125 feet.

Halted at about 3½ miles from the kand. This is hardly a place for troops, though they might manage to bivouac along the ravine. Water good and fairly abundant. Grass (*gurkao*) very plentiful on the hills. Wood and camel grazing moderate.

Warmer to-day and less wind.

Thursday, 18th February.—SAND. 15 miles. Elevation 2,820 feet.

From camp the nála widens. It is enclosed between cliffs of crumbling slate topped with conglomerate and looking like the scarps of plateaux. The descent is rapid at first.

At one mile a large nála comes in from left. Thence the kaur is 40 yards wide, the bounding scarps lower, and descent gradual. Its general direction is north-east, and it runs tolerably straight for a considerable distance.

At about 4¼ miles is some surface water. Immediately beyond is a leftward turn through a narrow but short defile. Here slaty rocks leave a practicable roadway only a yard or two wide, and the road is rough for a little way. The hills on either side are not more than 100 feet high, and easily accessible. This defile, like many similar places, is called Ábgir. Distance from second Whálí water 10¼ miles.

There is more water beyond the defile, and the nála again bends north-east. Road good.

At about 5¼ miles there is a southward bend round a small spur, and from thence the general direction is east. Road stony and not so good.

At about 6 miles leave the nála and turn left (north) up a small ravine. It is narrow and winds a good deal, but the road is good and hills quite insignificant.

At 7¼ miles cross a small kand. Thence descend another system of small ravines. The fall is considerable, and road in places narrow, but very fairly good.

At about 8¼ miles gain the Doráskí Kaur, a large watercourse, the main drainage channel of this part of the hills. It runs from about north-west to south-east. The route from Bela to Panjgúr through Áwárán, leads up this nála for a long way. Áwárán is two marches south-east.

About 200 yards above where the road from Málár comes in, is a rather small, but deep, perennial pool full of fish. It is known as the Zawardám Daf water, from the junction of the Zawardám being just below.

Here would be the second halting place from Málár; it is about 14 miles from the first halting place at Whálí second water. Could see no place to camp except the stony bed of the kaur, some 50 yards across. Water abundant and good. Wood, camel grazing, and grass moderate.

The guides had all along been declaring that they knew little of the road, and had only a vague general knowledge of the country beyond the Doráskí. In fact, the route by which we are travelling seems but little used or known. The Sirdar had given them directions, and they hoped to find the next camping place without much difficulty.

Following therefore Músa Khán's instructions, we crossed the Doráskí, and entering the Zawardám, proceeded up it. The general direction was about north-west by north nearly parallel to the Doráskí. The Zawardám is here a good width and tolerably straight. Hills on either hand quite low. The track is stony, but fair.

After about 1¼ miles the nála is somewhat contracted by a thin sheet, or wall, of rock. Immediately beyond this (10 miles) it is seen coming in on the north or north-north-west, and we quitted it, the track turning up a very small and insignificant nála on the left.

The latter soon widens to 10 yards with a gravel bottom. Road good. Ascending gradually through very low hills, we reached a watershed at about 11 miles. From thence a very easy and gently descending ravine of similar character was followed, at first in a westerly direction, and then south.

At about 12 miles this opened into a large kaur, which we all saw at once was the Doráskí, and it became evident that we had missed Músa Kháin's road, as indeed might have been expected.

Here we were fortunate enough to meet two Siahpád shepherds, the first people seen since leaving Málár, and after a talk decided on continuing up the Doráskí to the mouth of the Gwaní Nála, somewhere in which the proper halting place is situated, but evidently too far to be reached to-day with our half worn out animals.

Followed the kaur west-north-west. It is here about 80 yards wide, and increases rather than diminishes as it is ascended. Rise hardly perceptible. Plenty of písh and tamarisk in the bed, which is stony and not pleasant travelling; but the road is fair.

At about 15 miles ascended to, and crossed, a small bent on the right bank. Ascent and descent very easy. Not far beyond this we found a pool of water, and camped near it. The place is said to be called Sand.

Here wood and camel grazing were abundant; also *kasham* grass in the nála and *gurkao* on the hills. Water abundant and good. The pool is about 4 feet deep and 20 feet long. Only camping ground is the kaur itself, or the bent crossed lower down.

Cloudy and cold to-day.

Friday, 19th February.—RAVINE UNDER GWANÍ HILLS. 10 miles, marched 13. Elevation 3,747 feet.

Up the kaur west-north-west. Very soon it bends to right (north) Thence general direction north-west. Apparently a large plateau on the left : plateau and low hills on right.

At one mile is water under a scarp on the right. Thence northward. The nála bed is stony, and road not very good. The kaur now narrows to 50 yards, and there is water continuously for more than a quarter of a mile A plateau on the right 30 feet high. Might make a camping ground, but wood and camel grazing not so abundant as lower down.

The nála is now nearly straight for $1\frac{1}{2}$ miles. Near the top of this piece, on the left hand, is a very small ravine leading down from the plateau. It is called Azwí, and the spot is Azwí Daf. There should be water here, but we did not see any.

Above this (at $2\frac{1}{2}$ miles) the Doráskí bends away to left (west), and is joined by the Gwaní Kaur from the east.

Siháyandát, a gap or defile, is a little higher up the Doráskí. A rock over it is visible from Gwaní Daf, and appears about $\frac{3}{4}$ of a mile distant. Distance from Zawardám Daf to Siháyandát would therefore be between 9 and $9\frac{1}{2}$ miles.

The Panjgúr road leading up Doráskí was now quitted, and we turned to the right up the Gwaní Nála hoping to reach the foot of the Gwaní Kand The Siahpádí met yesterday said there was a halk or camp of 3 or 4 tents somewherew in this kaur, and I rather counted on getting a guide there. Sowars had also been sent back to catch one of the Síahpádís if possible.

The Gwaní leads in a general north-east direction. It is about 50 yards wide, rather increasing in width as ascended, and bounded by broken plateau and low hills. The bed of the nala is stony, and only a faint cattle track discernable.

After proceeding about two miles we caught sight of a man, a woman and a donkey. The trio perceiving us at the same moment at once fled up a small ravine to the plateau on the left. Here was an unexpected chance of getting a guide, or at least some information, so we dismounted and gave chase, but not all the blandishments of the Balúch sowars could prevail on any one of the three to return. The woman used her only weapon, *viz.*, her tongue, with much perseverance, while the man, lighting his match, retreated from one small eminence to another, vowing he would be the death of any one who approached him. It was then gravely suggested that I should show myself by way of convincing this hero that we were what we represented ourselves to be, and not Naoshírwánís. But even the sight of a terai hat and an ulster failed to inspire confidence, and we were obliged to continue our way without obtaining the desired interview.

At 6¾ miles the guide (*lucus a non lucendo*), after some hesitation, elected to leave the Gwaní and turn up another nála coming in from the north. A sort of a track leads up this nála, which is about 40 yards wide. Road very fair.

At 8 miles it narrows to about 20 yards. The sides are broken. From about here the ascent becomes very perceptible.

At 9 miles the nála wound through low clay slate hills. Its bed is filled with pish and small trees.

At 10 miles is water. The ascent is here considerable, but road good.

The guide now ascended a hill to spy out the land, and coming down announced that the nála was *band* or impracticable.

Somewhat doubting this I set off to walk and see. There is water for some distance up. The nála is about 10 yards wide and full of vegetation. It winds a good deal, and the hills on either side are high and steep.

After about 1½ miles a dyke of rock across the bed effectually stops the progress of any four footed animals except goats. We had evidently missed the road altogether.

I went on to the crest of the range,* a stiff walk of about 2½ miles further. From thence an extensive view over the hill country between Gitchk and Kólwáh. Kúlán peak was visible to the north-east, and Drún to the south-east. The Gwaní Kand is evidently some distance north-east or east-north-east, and it seems very doubtful if we shall ever reach it, as we have only two days grain. The ascent of this range will, however, be of some use from a surveying point of view.

Sent down and ordered baggage to unload at water, but they had already reached the impassable place, and had to retrace their steps.

The rumour of a large force coming down from Khárán seems to have frightened everybody out of this country. The sowars sent to catch one of the Siahpádís returned without having been able to find anybody.

A small tree bearing edible berries grows plentifully in the ravines of this range. It is called by the people "gwan," hence the name of the hills; but it is not the same as the well known gwan of Khurásán.

---

* Elevation estimated about 1,500 feet above camp, say 5,250 feet

Fine to-day and fortunately clear. Very cold on the top of the hill.
Saturday, 20th February.—ZAWARDÁM DAF. 16 miles. Elevation 2,718 feet.

Down the nála to its junction with the Gwání, 3 miles. Turned up the latter hoping to find the halk said to be somewhere here. The nála is of the same character and about the same size as before.

After going 2 miles (5 miles from camp) observed camel tracks coming out of a very narrow ravine on the right. Ascended a small hill to have a look round. No sign whatever of human life could be discerned, and probably the people formerly camped on this nála have departed to the south. The track in the ravine, however, could be seen for a little way, and appeared well marked and to lead towards Zawardám Daf—to be, in fact, the road by which we ought to have come, and I decided to take it.

The Gwání Kaur was observed running north-east up into the hills; but the ranges are somewhat intricate, and to find the pass without a guide might have taken us a week. It is a road that is very little used, and as a cattle track of some sort leads up every ravine, we might try a good many before hitting on the right one. Without a guide there was nothing for it but to find our back to Zawardám Daf, for which indeed we had to rely on such observations as I had been able to make from the crest of the range, as the guide (who had also been up there) declared himself perfectly confused, and declined to offer any opinion whatever.

Turned to right (south) up the small ravine. There is a little water close to the entrance. For some way it is enclosed between rocks, and is exceedingly narrow, but a laden camel can pass. After 100 or 150 yards more open.

The watershed is quickly gained, and from thence are two paths, one straight and the other leading down another small clay slate ravine to the south-west.

The latter had the well known sign of practicability,* so we took it, though with some misgiving.

The path was very good and led down into a somewhat larger watercourse, and so on, winding through small ranges, till a considerable nála was struck at about 2 miles (7 miles). We hoped this might be the Zawardám, and such it proved to be.

Continued to descend the kaur, which very much resembles all the others hereabouts, except that it led through hills rather than plateaux.

At about 4 miles (9 miles) to our great content it began to bend round south-east. Below this the bed is slate rock, rather rough, but not difficult for camels. Here there is abundant water, which is evidently perennial, and runs down for at least a mile.

The nála winds a good deal, but the general direction is south-east.

At 11 miles it passes the west end of the Zawardám Koh, a hill about 700 feet high with a flat top in the centre and small peak at each end—an unmistakable landmark. From thence the bed of the nála is more stony, and the road not quite so good. At 14 miles passed the place where we had quitted the nála two days before. Here there is a rather rough bit.

At 15½ reached the Doráski and turned down it. This kaur, running south-south-east, turns south about half a mile below the junction. Halted beyond

---

* A small pile of stones put on the top of one another. Stones laid in line across the track denote that it is *band*, or impracticable.

this near a good pool under the right bank. A bent on the left bank affords good camping ground for a detachment, and a larger bent just above would accommodate several battalions of native troops.

Wood, water, and camel grazing abundant. Grass from the hills moderate. Fine day; pleasantly warm.

Sunday, 21st February.—ĀWĀRĀN. 22 miles. Elevation 1,933 feet.

At first southwards, but the kaur soon turns rather to the left (east).

At 1¾ miles again south, but soon resumes an east-south-east course bending to east.

On the right is a cliff, about 400 feet high, called Doráskí Dát; the hill of which it is a scarp is known as the Doráskí Dát range.

At 2¾ miles turn south through this range, the kaur being narrowed to 50 yards. Its bed is very stony, but there is a tolerable path under the rocks on the right.

Below this the Pasáyan Nála comes in from the left (east-north-east) From hence is an extremely good bit of road over fine gravel to left of the nála bed.

At 4 miles bend round to south-west. At 4½ miles the kaur is contracted between scarps to a width of 40 yards. Road stony, but tolerable. Just below is a small pool on the left.

Thence bend south-east round to east. The road is stony. At 5½ miles turn to the right (south) and pass through a range.

The kaur now contracts, and at 6¼ miles is a short gorge, or gap, not more than 30 yards wide, by which the watercourse escapes through the main range, which on the right is called Askáni, and on the left Kandahár Koh.* The cliff on the Askáni side is 500 feet high, and that opposite not much less. There are perennial pools of water under the rocks.

From Zawardám Daf to this point the Doráskí has been making its way through successive narrow ranges in a general south-east direction. Each gap is 40 or 50 yards wide, but short. Between them the average width of the nála is 80 or 90 yards, and it is enclosed by scarps about 100 feet high. There is a good deal of tamarisk, &c., in places. The bed of the nála is stony, but road very fair.

On passing the main range the kaur runs east-north-east for a short distance. A spur of Askáni bounds it on the south. It then turns south, then east, bending south-east at 8 miles.

The Kándabar Koh is now seen towering on the left, and the kaur is very wide, a sort of basin being formed by the confluence of nálas from the hill.

At 8½ miles the kaur turns south leaving the high hills. Its breadth is 80 to 100 yards, and it is enclosed by scarps of no great height, which are soon succeeded by low ridges parallel to the main range.

For about 2½ miles its course is fairly straight. The track disappears here and travellers pick their way over the stones according to individual fancy.

At 11 miles there is a rock on the right noticeable for two miles back. is called Tírtejh, and there should be abundant water at its foot. We found, however, very little showing. Probably the last flood shifted the gravel so as to nearly choke the pool. There is plenty below the surface.

---

* The Khandahár Koh is said to be so called because it is high enough to be occasionally covered with snow in winter; and t us, according to the ideas of the Mekráns, resembles the hills about Kandahár, which is imagined to be an exceedingly cold place.

As this spot is midway between Áwárán and Zawardám Daf, it is commonly made a halting place by travellers, but I could see no place to pitch a camp. Grass is very scanty. Wood and camel grazing abundant.

From Tirtejh the kaur turns sharp to the right (west), but soon again south, and at 11¼ miles passes through a gap in a small range. Deep holes on the right were quite dry.

Thence leave the kaur and, ascending the right bank, strike south-west along a sort of valley a mile wide between two parallel ridges. This way is rather longer than following the watercourse, but better going.

At 13½ miles gain the Bázáp Nála, and follow it south through the ridge hitherto on the left. The Bázáp is a considerable watercourse thickly grown with tamarisk. In fact, the amount of jungle makes it difficult to tell the exact point where the Doráskí is re-entered. The latter is now a quarter of a mile wide and runs south-south-east. Confused low hills on both sides.

There is no track here, but it seems best to keep near the right bank. Water in several places. It would appear that if the water under Tirtejh rock is insufficient, a good supply may be counted on not more than two miles lower down, and a camping ground might be formed on some neighbouring plateau.

There is *drab* grass in the nála. Wood and camel grazing abundant.

At 15½ miles turn to the left and leave the kaur. A well marked track now leads through low rocky hills, winding here and there, but having a general easterly direction.

At 17¼ miles a very low kotal is crossed. At the foot of the ascent is a path leading from Bázdár, 10 or 11 miles south-west of Áwárán, inside the outer hills, to Gwarjak and Gajar.

At last the hills become mere gravel undulations. From the very last there is a considerable descent, at 19¼ miles, to the plain, which is here partially cultivated.

The Mírwárí hamlet of Mulla Murád is left on the right at 21 miles.

Áwárán is reached at 22. It was long after dark when we got there, and we learnt that the baggage, arriving about sunset, nearly had a warm reception, as the people of Áwárán were expecting an attack, and took our party for enemies.

Fine, pleasant day.

Monday, 22nd February.—Halted. Surveying. Went about 6½ miles on the Bázdár road (south-west). The Doráskí in several stony channels is crossed at 2 miles. Here jungle of tamarisk and accacia is thick. A long and deep pool in the kaur where the road crosses. Thence through jungle, gradually getting thinner; low rocky hills running parallel on the left. The tree jungle is interspersed with large open spaces grown with drab grass. There are many pig in this country. We saw their rootings right away up in the Zawardám Nála.

Bázdár has a fort on a mound, round which are some 70 or 80 huts of Bízanjaos. Water from wells. There is a good deal of khushkáwa cultivation in the neighbourhood.

Áwárán is a fort of the ordinary description built on a mound. The walls are high and carefully loopholed. There is one large tower. The whole appears to be in very good repair. One well inside the fort and three out. Around are clustered some 80 huts of Bízanjaos. This place belongs to Safar Khán, brother of Mír Kaliíra, Bízanjao chief and naib of Mekrán. Safar Khán is now at Nál collecting a force to oppose the Mírwárís and their Naoshírwání allies. Azím Khán, son of his first cousin, was in charge of the fort and did the honours. His own son Hasil Khán is recently dead of a wound received in the affair at Rodakán in November last (1881). See page 69.

A certain amount of land about Áwárán is watered by a stream from the Mashkai Kaur. Wheat is cultivated, but barley is the principal crop. Grass is difficult to procure, being brought from a long way. We got *kasíl*, and bhúsa would be procurable after the harvest.

Mulla Murád is a small fort and hamlet of about 20 huts one mile north-west of Áwárán. The people are Mírwárís. There is one well inside the fort and two outside. The land is watered by the same stream from the Mashkaí Kaur that irrigates Áwárán, and there is said to be a karez to the west.

There are no bannias permanently resident in Áwárán, nor indeed were there any in Kólwáh, though there happens to be one now at Bédí. Many bannias, however, visit the district in spring and summer to purchase wood and ghi. A little grain is also exported.

Both Bízanjaos and Mírwárís own very large numbers of sheep and goats, which find good pasturage in the surrounding hills. Horned cattle are also fairly numerous.

Bédí is a fort and village of about 40 huts of Mírwárís, three-quarters of a mile north-east by east of Áwárán, on the left bank of the Mashkai Kaur, whose stony shallow channels fill up the whole space between the villages. There are three wells here. Bédí belongs to, and is one of the residences of, Mír Abdul Karím, Mírwárí chief and naib of Kolwáh and Mashkai. He is now in Khárán —*i. e.*, by latest report he was at Nágha Kalát,—waiting to hear from Azád Khán. His son Malik Dínár is in charge of the fort with a strong garrison, but the familes of the people ordinarily residing here have been removed.

One banaia at Bédí. This man, a native of Karáchí and British subject, was very desirous of proceeding with me to Hingól, but Malik Dínár would not suffer him to depart.

Tuesday, 23rd February.—MANGULI 25 miles. Elevation 2,625 feet.

The first thing this morning we heard that Malik Dínár of Bédí, had made a raid on Bázdár during the night and carried off some camels. All the men of Áwárán had consequently gone out to lie in wait round Bédí and endeavour to intercept the plunder as it was brought in, and Azím Khán sent to say we should have to wait a little for our guides and camel men. These, however, turned up before long, as it had been discovered that the plunderers were too knowing to return to Bédí and had made off up the Doráskí Kaur.

Azím Khán now informed us that he had received certain intelligence of the Naoshírwání force, which would be here in three days, and he positively declined to allow his camels or men to go on up Kólwáh. He would send them with us as far as Jao on the Hingól road, but nowhere else.

As it was absolutely necessary for me to go on up to Tank-ná-káh, this sudden resolution on the part of Azím Khán was somewhat perplexing. I could not, however, but agree that the risk to the Bízanjaos and their cattle was serious, as it is all Mírwárí country to the north-east, and that to protect them and the camels we might ourselves be drawn into a fight. Had Abdul Karím been present some arrangement might have been come to, but no assistance could be expected from Malik Dínár. Besides it was almost impossible to wait even for one day, supplies being most difficult to procure. Azím Khán, expecting to be shortly besieged, was naturally anxious to save what he had, and made a favour of allowing us 10 days flour and 4 or 5 days grain. I thought at the time that the report of the Naoshírwánís being down in three days was probably a polite fiction to get us away as soon as possible, and such I believe it to have been

After some little talk it was settled that the baggage should go to Álam Khán's village in Jao and wait there, while I, with four sowars, was to make a "daur" to Tank, and thence straight to Jao, Azím Khán furnishing one camel sowar to show us the road.

While making our hasty preparations, I received visits from Mír Mandao Khán, Bízanjao, of Chambúr, and Mulla Murád, Mírwárí, whose hamlet of the same name is close by. The former is a very aged man, nearly blind, and just able to walk with the aid of a staff. Yet he had come here to take part in the contest with the Mírwárís. Mandao Khán was for long naib of Urmára, and appears to have been popular and respected, both with the people and with such British officials as have known him.

Owing to the various delays, it was half past eleven before we started. The party consisted of the Rasaldar and three Balúch sowars, on the four mares which alone remained serviceable out of twelve; one Sind Horse sowar; and myself on a camel, both my mares being unfit to go. A servant with bedding was on the second riding camel. We could only take two days provisions, but hoped to rejoin the rest of the party in three or four days.

The Mashkaí Kaur leaves the hills some miles north of Áwárán, and its flood waters cross the plain by numerous channels, extending over at least a mile in width, and forming a sheet of shingle covered with thin jungle. The bed is quite dry, all water being drawn off for irrigation purposes.

Two roads lead north-eastwards from Áwárán. The first skirts the right bank of the kaur and enters the hills by the gap from which it issues. Thence it leads most of the way through low rocky hills, leaving the kaur to the left. It is said to be a good road and somewhat the most direct of the two. The other route goes north-east across the stony expanse of the Mashkai Kaur, past Bélí, to Pírandar Kalát, the latter being a small Mírwárí fort and village about 3 miles from Áwárán. There are wells here, one inside the fort and one outside.

We took the latter route. At Pírandar we crossed the high road from Bélá to Panjgúr. It traverses the plain diagonally and quits it by the Mashkai gap, from whence it leads west or west by north to the Doráskí Kaur (see Routes). Continuing by a good road up the valley we reached, at 8 miles, a place called Púndú. Here there is a good deal of cultivation, watered by the flood of the Púndú Kaur, but no village. The Kolwáh plain is now rather narrower than at Áwárán. It lies north-east and south-west, and does not curve up northwards to Mashkai as anticipated. The people here are Mírwárís.

The road now bends north-north-east. At $9\frac{1}{2}$ miles passed a well. It is about 100 feet deep and contains plenty of water. There is another well in Púndú, some distance to the east.

At $11\frac{1}{2}$ miles enter low hills. General direction of road north-north-east. At $12\frac{1}{2}$ miles cross a clay slate ridge to the basin of the Dránkolí nála, which runs out to the plain close by.

Turn north by west up the Dránkolí. There is another road, apparently straighter, but it crosses a difficult kand said to be impracticable for laden camels. Small rocky ranges are soon entered, and the road, following a watercourse, winds north-west, and then north. At 13½ miles cross a small kand, on this side (south) of which there is a little water. This spot is supposed to be exactly half way between Áwárán and Manguli.

From the kand turn south-west, for a short distance between ridges, then round the end of that on the right, and proceed north-east over a narrow plateau, soon descending to the Púndú Kaur, which here runs south-west, in a bed about 40 yards wide and 60 feet deep, between low ranges.

Thence ascend the Púndú in a north-easterly direction. Good road.

At about 16 miles cross a bent, and having descended again to the kaur follow it north-north-west through the left hand range. This being cleared the former direction is resumed.

A wider valley is now traversed. It is broken by low hills and undulations through which the lessening nála is followed; the road being sometimes in its bed, but mostly on the right bank.

At 18¾ miles cross the watershed. On the further side the drainage is to the Kanéro Nála.

The road now approaches the left hand range, which is reached at 19¼ miles. The path descends into the Kanéro and follows it down through the ridge. Here there is a waterhole, and in a small ravine on the north-west side of the hill, a short distance to right of the road, is abundant water. The place is known as Kanéro.

A track from the upper part of Kolwáh above Púndú joins in at the gap.*

The Kanéro is now followed west-north-west. At 20¾ miles, having crossed a bent, descend to to the kaur, where it passes through another range, and immediately cross over to the right bank, inclining north-east, while the nála goes away north-west.

At 21¼ miles descend to a small watercourse. Here the other road from Áwárán joins in.

At 22 miles cross a watershed, which marks the boundary between Kolwáh and Mashkai.

At 22¼ miles turn to left and descend into the Lagúr Nála, where it passes through another of the numerous small parallel ranges. It goes away north-west, like the Kanéro, and is quitted at once.

At 23¼ miles bend half left, and half a mile further enter close parallel ranges bordering on the Mashkai Kaur, between which the road runs for a short distance north-east.

At 24¼ miles turn to the left through the second range and descend through a small rocky defile about a third of a mile in length. It opens on to the Mashkai stream, here running in a narrow broken valley. The further bank is reached at 25 miles, and Manguli fort and hamlet are a few hundred yards further on, to the right.

There is a certain amount of cultivation here watered from the Mashkai (which it should be remembered is higher up known as the Dhuléri).

The fort belongs to Abdul Karím. It is of the usual type, standing on a low mound, with a large square tower, below which are two small yards. The walls are of rubble, mortared with mud, and loopholed. They are of the rudest construction, but high and in good repair. The fort is commanded within matchlock range by low hills to the north-west. About 30 huts were standing near, but the whole place was perfectly deserted. There is no well in the fort,

---

* We took this road in returning from Manguli.

but one close to outside; also a ruined watermill to the south-east. Ground might be found for encampment to the south-west. Wood and camel grazing abundant. Grass in hills, but none near at hand. Some bhusa and grain would be procurable after the harvest in April or May. Mangulí is in the Mashkaí district, Kolwáh having been left at the Kanéro watershed.

It was quite dark when we reached Mangulí. We quartered ourselves in the empty fort, and as the place seemed perfectly deserted, I allowed the sowars to cut some kasíl from the nearest field for the tired and hungry horses, the Rasaldar remarking at the time that we had a right to *mehmdní*, or hospitality, from so great a man as Abdul Karím.

The road is good all the way from Awárán. It is said to be rather better than the other road and very little longer. Troops would halt at Púndú. There is a track right down the kaur, but it is said to be very stony, and not so good as either of the others.

Wednesday, 24th February.—To TANK-NA-BÁH and back. 21¾ miles.

Early in the morning some men made their appearance and requested us not to cut any more kasíl, offering to bring us grass if paid for it. This was of course acceded to, and I may as well add that the grass was brought in the evening and paid for at their own price.

Leaving my servant and one sowar in the fort with directions to purchase some grain if they could, we started for Tank-ná-báh; that is, the junction of the Tank stream with the Dhulérí or Mashkaí, below Gwarjak; down to which point I had carried the reconnaissance survey, and up to which it was necessary to go to join on the former work, besides which my instructions included an exploration of the route from Gwarjak, southwards, to Hingól on the sea.

The road north-east from Mangulí leads from the north of the fort through the low hills on the right bank (north-west) of the stream. These are backed by the high range called Kúrmí, which joins the Kandahár Kóh to Surgarh, south-west of the Tank defile, and forms part of the long chain extending from the watershed between Kodak and Besemar to Kej.

There is another road up the valley, and I elected to take this first. Crossing the stony and jungle grown bed of the Kúrmí Nála, we skirted a conglomerate plateau abutting on the stream. On one of the bluffs are the remains of an old Mírwárí fort called Sháhjai.

The Mashkai has a broad, stony, and shallow bed partly grown with jungle. The running stream is small, not greater than at Gajar, a good deal of water being drawn off for cultivation. All the cultivation lies on the right bank. Just above Mangulí it bends from south-south-west to south-west.

At about 2¾ miles passed cultivation called Dairoh.

At 4 miles the Hírání Nála joins the Mashkai from the north-east. The high range beyond, a continuation of that bounding the Mashkai valley proper on the east, is also called Hírání.

Opposite to Hírání junction are fields called Gazí. Above these is more cultivation called Gúrkí. These places all belong to Mírwárís. There are no permanent habitations, but a very fair population of tent people (including some Muhammad Hasánís) and numerous flocks were met with.

At about 5½ miles an insignificant watercourse was pointed out as the division between Mírwárís and Sájdís. The latter thenceforward extend up to Gwarjak, which is Naoshírwání. Beyond this nála the road first mentioned joins in from behind the low hills.

The first Sájdí fields are called Búndaki. Above these, but on the opposite side, the Sinkúri Nála joins the Mashkai. It contains a perennial stream. A short distance higher up low hills close on the kaur, and the track winds through those on the right bank.

At 8 miles, having rejoined the kaur, reach the kafila halting place of Shíringaz at the lower end of cultivation of the same name. The fields extend in patches for about a mile and a quarter.

Hence for 2½ miles, or more, up to Tank-ná-báh, the Mashkai is a broad defile. We stopped and ascended a low hill about a mile short of the junction.

Returning, took the proper road through the hills. It appears to be about half a mile shorter, and is much the best, as the other is continually impeded by water channels, cultivation, and jungle.

From Mangulí fort through the low hills to Búndakí cultivation on the kaur is about 5½ miles. Thence to Tank-ná-báh, 6 miles. Total 11½ miles.

Found that the sowar had succeeded in buying about 15 seers of barley, which was all he could get. It transpired afterwards that the young man had *bought*, but not paid for, a lamb from a passing flock. He said the lad in charge ran away. This I did not know of till next day.

Thursday, 25th February.—Halted. Was awakened during the night by my surwan rushing up from below and calling out that one of the two riding camels had been stolen. The horses and camels were in the lower yard, and two sowars and the surwan slept with them. The space was only about large enough to contain the lot comfortably. Nevertheless a camel had been taken away, passing within a foot of these three men's heads. Sobat Khán the Rasaldar, and all the men at once rushed out into the darkness, leaving me to mount sentry till they returned, somewhat crestfallen, in about half an hour, and of course without having done any good. I then directed Sobat Khán to send round quietly to two or three small camps that we had discovered were in the neighbourhood, and see if any news could be picked up. The guide and two men started at once, and at daybreak the Rasaldar reported that near one of the camps they had heard a number of men moving, and on challenging them the latter had taken to a small hill and lighted their matches. Some parley then ensued, in which the men aforesaid declared with much warmth that we had been behaving very badly in cutting crops and in taking the lamb (this was the first I heard of the latter). The guide recognised the voice of a certain Muhammad Hasání called Murád, and had gone with one of our men to fetch him if possible.

About an hour later Murád with several men was reported to have arrived, but they declined to come near the fort. Sobat Khán accordingly went to talk to them.

After a time I thought it better to see what was taking place. Murád was a villanous looking old scoundrel, and decidedly insolent in his demeanour. He had four men with him, all armed with matchlock and talwar, &c. Sobat Khán and the Balúch guide sowars were furious, and I had to exert my authority to prevent them attacking the robbers, for such no doubt they were.

Being six well armed men, besides the guide, who was delighted at the prospect of a shindy, we could easily have fallen on Murád's camp, of at the most 15 or 20 raggamuffins, and made them pay very dearly for the night's amusement; and according to the custom of the country this would have been the proper thing to do. Of course all the Mírwárís in the neighbourhood, who looked upon us more or less in the light of enemies from having a Bízanjao guide, would have joined, and there would have been a very pretty *tamasha*.

Unfortunately British officers cannot right themselves in this manner and in the present instance it would not have fulfilled the primary object of getting back the camel, which had doubtless been driven away into the hills. Provoking as it was, therefore, to be bearded by such scum, I was obliged to say there could be no fighting. After a good deal of talk about the kasfl and the lamb, Murád said he would go and *look for* the camel, if I would give him Rs. 10 for its recovery.

This was promised, and he departed, saying he would return by midday. We now thought the camel would be restored, and set ourselves to wait with as much patience as possible.

About eleven our watch was enlivened by the appearance of some dozen matchlock men, whose leader gave his name as Ghulám Alí, and said he was a Mírwárí and retainer of Abdul Karím. Having heard that I had lost a camel, he had collected a few men and come to *assist in its recovery*. This disinterested conduct, however, was quite lost on Sobat Khán, who refused further parley, and wanted to open fire on the new arrivals, declaring they had simply come to keep us where we were during Murád's absence. After some time, Ghulám Alí, from a distance, bellowed a humble request to be allowed to come in and talk. He and one man were admitted, and the pipe of peace went round. It was at once discovered, as indeed we all along imagined, that the fields belonged to Abdul Karím, and any claim to compensation for damage could only be made by the Mírwárís, and certainly not by Murád. The latter however, was actually the proprietor of the lamb.

About two o'clock Murád returned without the camel, saying he was afraid we might attack his tuman if he stayed longer. He had left men on the tracks of the animal, and it would no doubt be brought in by night. Ghulám Alí also professed to believe that the camel would certainly be brought back. I was now fairly disgusted, and would have marched; but Sobat Khán was of opinion that these delays were only intended to enhance the reward for recovery, and that the camel would make its appearance if we stayed till next morning. As the beast with his saddle was worth Rs. 100, and his loss was besides a great inconvenience, I agreed to wait.

Much talk, to which I paid no attention, went on during the afternoon and evening. Sobat Khán, an excellent young man, and himself of Sirdar's rank was extremely irate at the indignity that had been put upon us; and I heard him abusing all the Jhálawáns from the time of Kambar downwards, and explaining how impossible it would have been for such a thing to happen in *his* country. About 10 at night he reported that Murád had acknowledged to Ghulám Alí having possession of the camel, and plainly said he wanted Rs. 50 to give it back. By degrees this sum diminished to Rs. 20, and compensation for the lamb and kasfl. It was now quite evident that Ghulám Alí and Murád were acting together in a barefaced attempt to extort money from a *sahib*, who appeared too weak to offer resistance. Of course I declined to give one farthing more than the Rs. 10 originally promised.

Previous to this I had told Ghulám Alí that if, as Abdul Karím's representative, he wished to be of assistance, I would be obliged to him to let me have a camel for hire to replace the one stolen. He declared his willingness to give us one for nothing, and also volunteered a statement to the effect that it was absurd to talk about compensation for the few handfuls of kasíl. I now sent to say I should march in the morning, and to request the camel might be forthcoming at an early hour.

Friday, 26th February.—NÚNDARA. 24 miles. Elevation 1,675 feet, Marched at 8-45, having waited some time for Ghulám Ali's camel, which never appeared. I insisted upon that individual taking a rupee for the kasíl, and also gave him Rs. 2, which he might hand over to Murád for the lamb. Murád himself with a few men was sitting on a hillock a short distance off. He hoped perhaps to get something out of us, and the Rasaldar thought some resistance would probably be offered to our departure.

As we had been so peaceful yesterday, this was possible, but nothing took place. I think we were all a little disappointed in consequence.

The above incident has been noted in detail, because it shows in how false a position a British officer places himself when he travels, as such, in a perfectly lawless country without a proper escort. The character of the Balúch and Bráhúis seems to be somewhat misunderstood. They are perfectly devoid of fanaticism, and have none of the rancorous hate of the Afghán towards an Englishman and an infidel. On the contrary, they greatly respect, and even like, the British, and the vast majority of the chiefs may be relied upon to protect a British officer, under most circumstances, to the best of their ability. It must not be forgotten, however, that all, both small and great, are freebooters by inclination and practice. There is no more order, or security for life and property, in Balúchistán, generally, than in Afghánistán; and though a British officer need have no care for his personal safety, he is almost certain to be plundered sooner or later unless his belongings are properly protected. These opinions are the result of an experience extending over ten years, and embracing almost the whole country. Our party consisted of 15 fighting men, including myself, and we were strong enough to take care of each other in almost any conceivable situation. The moment, however, I was compelled to travel with only four or five men loss was suffered, and that in a way calculated to provoke a breach of the peace.

We followed the road by which we had come for about six miles, and then, instead of leaving the Kanéró Nála, which we entered on the outward journey we went on up it, bending somewhat round to the right.

At eight miles crossed a watershed, and thence turned to the left, following a very narrow little ravine through a small ridge. Beyond this is a second watershed, and a view is obtained of the upper end of Kólwáh, unexpectedly far below, with sloping *dámán* and insignificant looking bare hills beyond.

Descent is by a clay slate ravine, narrow, but a good road. After about a mile of rather rapid descent, turn to the right, crossing small clay slate undulations, and gain a larger ravine, which is followed south-west.

At 10¼ miles is water. It is abundant and good, but I could see no place where it would be possible to camp. The place is called Gutén Kanéro.

Thence turn to the left and follow the watercourse through the outer range. It is single and soon passed. Immediately afterwards bend round to the right (south) and cross the plain diagonally. It is entirely stony, covered with bushes and thin jungle, and devoid of cultivation. To south-west the fields of Púndú are not far. In the opposite direction the valley stretches for apparently over 20 miles to the foot of a range called Manjao, which seems to run nearly north and south, and is a continuation of the hills east of Jibrí The width of the valley is about 4 miles.

At about 13 miles cross the Chíl Nála, which carries the drainage of upper Kólwáh to the Doráskí. Thence a gradual ascent. At 14 miles enter the Chigardí Nála, and follow its course south-south-west.

At 15½ miles the track is close under, and east of, the dark isolated rock called Garók, which is a landmark all over this part of Kólwah.

Thence cross a small watershed, and at about 16 miles enter the Káshí Nála, which runs westward, and is soon quitted.

At 17 miles enter the Gaz Nála, so called from a large tamarisk tree a few hundred yards higher up. There is a little water not far from the tree to left of the road. In the Gaz the high road to Bélá is struck and followed up the nála. In less than a mile the foot of an unimportant looking range is reached, and there is an easy ascent to a kand called Barikí, the crest of which is gained at 18 miles.

Here again one is surprised to find oneself on the brink of a considerable descent. The track leads down a narrow and rough ravine. The fall here is very rapid, and the ascent must be decidedly trying for laden camels. Water soon appears, and runs down the ravine for some distance. Except the very small amount in the Gaz Nála, this is the only perennial source between Gutén Kanéro and the Jao valley.

At 19½ miles the water ceases and the ravine becomes easy. Between this and the crest it would be very difficult to make a road practicable for artillery.

At 20½ miles clear the hill and enter Núndara, but it is some little way down the *dámán* before the actual plain is reached.

Thence about south-east by east, bending east-south-east, over very light and soft alluvial soil, rising into clouds of dust at every step. Somewhat thick jungle of tamarisk, accacia, and ber trees covers the plain.

At 24 miles reached the Núndara Kaur, which is nearly at the opposite side of the valley. Here we bivouacked. Water, from a large rainpool, very muddy, but abundant. The supply is of course precarious; still there is nearly always water here; and, if not, it could doubtless be obtained by digging. Wood and camel grazing most abundant. *Drab* grass also abundant; better grass could be obtained from the hills a mile or less to the south.

Núndara is a large valley. To the south-west it goes as far as the Doráskí, probably 7 or 8 miles. To the north-east it extends an indefinite distance. Its width is 5 or 6 miles. It is really well wooded, and the ground is covered with láni and other scrub. Some 6 miles north-east of our bivouac are two small forts and hamlets of Mírwárís about a mile apart, and known as Núndara Kalát. There is a good deal of khushkáwa land in the neighbourhood. The people drink from wells. Here is the residence of Jalál Khán, chief of Núndara. The place is deserted at present owing to the Bízanjao war. This country is exclusively Mírwárí; the Rodéni, Sumakírí, and Gúrganárí sections are represented.

There is a road up Núndara to Nál (see Route No. XVII B).

Unless the water at Gutén Kanéro could be brought down outside the hills, which is improbable, troops marching northward would have to diverge to the Púndú wells (about 12 or 13 miles from here), and thence march to Mangulí (15½ miles) by the route taken on the 23rd.

The weather, which has been fine and clear since leaving Áwárún, suddenly turned thick and misty to-day. The mist came up so suddenly that I had only just time to take some necessary bearings in Kólwáh before the hills were obliterated.

Saturday, 27th February.—JAO (ÁLAM KHAN's VILLAGE). 23 miles. Elevation 1,350 feet.

Started east by south from the kaur, still following the Béla road. Low hills are soon entered, and the track bending rather to east, ascends to a small kand, the crest of which is reached at about 1 mile. Descent slightly rough into a small valley called Garistán, which appears to join Núndara to the west.

Crossing this, pursue a winding course about east-south-east, ascending steadily through low hills.

At 5 miles is a kand called Kánlári. Very easy ascent, and on gaining the top, which is somewhat flat, turn to the right for a short distance. Descent by an excellent road down a broad ravine through low hills. General direction south-east or south-east by east.

After some distance turn to the left up a broad affluent nála. The Kándárí goes away to the right (south-west.)

This watercourse is soon left, and turning to the right there is a gentle ascent to a watershed (7 miles). Descent easy through low hills in the original east-south-easterly direction.

Thence turn left (east) along the course of the Bodero Kaur. At about 9 miles bend slightly to left (east by north) parallel to the Sér hills, which flank the Bodero to the south.

At 9½ miles, a little to the right of the road, is some water and the kafila halting place of Bodero. The water-supply is scanty, but possibly more might be got by digging. There is room to camp on low plateaux bordering the nála. Pish would afford fuel, but there is no camel grazing. Some grass on the hills, but not much. Such as it is, this is the only halting place for troops between Jao and Núndara.

From the water, follow the nála eastward to the foot of the Sér Kand, a pass over the hills of the same name.

A good and short ascent up the hill side to the crest, which is reached at 10½ miles. It is considered to be half way to the kafila halting place of Jao, which must be considerably to the east or north-east of Álam Khán's village.

The descent is also fairly easy. At first down a small ravine; a larger one called Katú is soon entered, and followed first east, and then south, through a gap in the second Sér range. The gap is narrow, but afterwards the kaur widens to 50 yards, and is still followed south-east through low hills. After about 1½ miles it turns more to the south.

At 13 or 13½ miles the Makí Nála joins from the left. Thence the Katú winds through hills and becomes a defile. The road from Núndara kalat j ins in from the left. After this the nála bends south by west to pass through a comparatively considerable range about 600 feet high. The gap or gorge is short, but only 30 yards wide. Here there is a rain-water pool under the rock on the left hand. Below is more water, which runs a little.

The pass is now much wider and winds round south-east, and then east.

At 15 miles turn south-east through the last of the Sér ranges. Immediately the *dámán* is reached, the track turns due south, quitting the Bela road, which goes on south-east.

The path is indistinct and is soon lost altogether, but the *dámán* is good travelling. Slaty gravel and shingle with thin jungle.

At 17½ miles, when close to the edge of the alluvial soil, strike a path leading parallel to it and to the hills (south-west).

At about 20 miles, having left the *dámán*, skirt cultivation on the left. Half a mile further turn south past the end of these fields.

At 21½ miles strike the right bank of the Nálí Kaur, a stream running in a very large bed. The bank is a perpendicular scarp 50 or 60 feet deep, and the descent is steep and difficult. The flowing water is about 15 yards across and 18 inches deep, with a gentle current. Ford good, the bottom being of firm sand.

Thence parallel to the left bank through a wood of large tamarisks to the Bízanjao hamlet of Máhmud, 22 miles.

Turning to the right, just before reaching this, we regained the river bed by an easy descent and crossed it. The ford is good, but deeper than the first.

The hamlet of Álam Khán, Mírwárí, on the right bank, a little lower down than Mahmud's village, is reached at 23 miles.

Here we found our camp, which had arrived two days before, all well.

The valley of Jao is very large. It lies north-east and south-west. To the northward are hills of considerable height (from this side) known as Gabaróh, Pílarí Band, Gazí, &c. On the south or south-east side are conglomerate plateaux having a gentle slope towards Jao, but presenting a lofty scarped face in the opposite direction. Including gravel slopes on either hand, the width of the valley may be taken at 8 or 9 miles. Its length is more difficult to determine. From Álam Khán it appears to stretch at least 20 miles south-west, and at that end it is traversed by the Mashkai Kaur. North-east the direct extension of the valley is filled by undulating gravel plateaux similar to those on the south, and is not considered as part of Jao proper. However, the country is open for a long way, and here runs the road to Urnách. This part is bounded on the north-west by a long range called Lárandárí, which appears to lie on the same line as the hills north of Jao. But between Lárandarí and Gazí is a wide gap, north-north-east of Álam Khán, and through this the plain extends north-east to a range considerably more distant than those above mentioned. Here it is called Pelár, and is part of Jao.

The Nálí Kaur, or stream of Nál,* runs through Pelár and the gap, past Álam Khán, in a general westerly direction, and uniting with the Maskhai to form the Hingól river goes southward through defiles called Sor.

From Pelár on the north-east to Sor on the south-west is said to be six camel stages, or three days ride, and the distance can hardly, therefore, be less than 70 miles.

Beyond the gravel plateaux, but distant from the southern scarp some 10 or 12 miles, is an enormous mass of sandstone called Drún. Its highest part is due south of Álam Khán. This is about the centre; the westward portion is much lower, and it is round the extreme west end that the river escapes. To the east-north-east Drún is continued by a similar mountain called Wáshapí and north-east of Wáshapí, but apparently at some little distance, is Kachao, which flanks the Urnách road.

Arah is a cultivated valley between Wáshapí and Kachao. It belongs to Jangí Bízanjaos, and the road to Bálá runs through it. It is drained by the

---

* Also called here the Jao Kaur. It has a very large bed, at least 100 yards across and 50 feet deep. The banks are alternately scarped and shelving. The running stream is ordinarily 15 yards across, shallow, and rather sluggish. The water is good.

Arah Kaur, which runs south-west and passes through a defile between Wáshapí and Drún. By this defile is the road to Hingól.

Drún and Wáshapí are both tablelands, or rather perhaps they contain large *thals*, or basins, that in a more moist climate would be mountain lakes. These upland plains are cultivated (khushkáwa),* and there are said to be springs on both hills. Drún is much the largest, and is described as being half a march wide from north to south, and a full march long from east to west. The land on Drún belongs to Álam Khán, Mirwárí. There is but one tolerable path up to it, from the Arah Kaur gorge, and this is only practicable for donkeys. There is also a footpath called Chák from the west. Elsewhere the frowning scarps are inaccessible, except in rare instances, and to a practised mountaineer. To the summit of Wáshapí, however, there is a camel track from the Béla road.

Both Drún and Wáshapí are said to literally swarm with ibex, but there are very few oorial, these animals preferring lower ground. The small hill leopard also abounds.

Besides the road to Mashkai crossing upper Kólwáh, there are two roads to Awárán. One is the Ziárát road (see Routes); the other leads over the Gab-aróh Kand, but it is a bad road and impracticable for laden camels.

There are no forts in Jao, and no villages properly so called. Small collections of huts are, however, numerous, and the country may be considered well populated. There is a good deal of khushkáwa cultivation, especially to the north-east in Pelár, &c., but no irrigation, the people being incompetent to raise the water of the Nálí Kaur from its deep bed.

The country is really well wooded; in fact, along the banks of the kaur there is almost a forest of tamarisk, accacia, bér, &c. Láni and other low country scrub is abundant; so that Jao much resembles some portions of Sind. Large flocks of sheep and goats are seen everywhere, both in the valley and on the surrounding hills. The people also own cattle and a great number of camels, the country being well suited to the latter.

North-east of the Béla road the inhabitants are exclusively Bízanjaos, the following sections being represented:—

Umarári, chief man		Fakír.
Hamalárí	„	Lál Khán.
Chanál	„	Mír Dost.
Ninduwári	„	Aládáh.

To south-west of the same line, the land belongs to Mirwarís, whose head is Álam Khán, but they are rayats of Mír Kahíta, and all Jao is included in the "ráj" of that chief.

Jao is in the province of Jhálawán, and not in Mekrán. It is considered to belong to Nál.

Sunday, 28th February.—Áogháxí. 7¼ miles. Elevation 1,732 feet.
Should have liked to halt a day, but hearing it was farther to Hoag than had been supposed determined to move on.

Crossed the river and turned down the left bank. General direction south-east through thickly wooded and somewhat broken ground. Very soft soil.

---

* Excellent jowari is grown on Drun, besides mel us, &c. † About 100 men.

At about 1½ miles bend east. Here the country is more open, but still thickly studded with trees, mostly accacia. After another mile inclined east-south-east, the trees getting smaller and further apart.

At 3¼ miles entered a bare gravel tract, ascending slightly. After quarter of a mile strike a track leading south-east. This is the Bélá road apparently coming straight across the valley from where we left it yesterday on quitting the hills. To go to Álam Khán is therefore a detour, but not a very long one.

At 4¼ miles bend east-south-east. Very gradual, but steady, ascent. Good road. At 5½ miles quit the Bélá road, and follow an indistinct track south-east. Soon after there is a slight descent into a hollow, 500 yards wide, of alluvial soil and grown with bushes.

Another similar hollow is crossed soon afterwards. These drain west, and meet after a short distance.

At 6¾ miles bend south-east. The bare gravel plateau is now decidedly undulating.

At 7 miles cross a small ravine called Sor (salt). It is a branch of the Áogháni, and contains a little brackish water.

The Áogháni ravine is struck almost immediately afterwards. Rather an awkward little descent, but ascent easy. We camped on the further side. Water fairly abundant in the ravine, and it is of good quality, but considerably befouled by the sheep and goats, which appear to be continually being brought here to water. However, one or two small holes seem to be purposely kept clean for drinking purposes.

There is no good ground for camping close to the water, but no doubt a tolerable site might be found at no great distance. Wood and camel grazing procurable, but not plentiful. Some *gurkao* grass.

We stopped here, as there is no water nearer than the Arah Kaur, a long way ahead.

Fairly good view of the surrounding country. In no part of Sárawán, Jhálawán, or Mekrán, is there so large a space devoid of high hills.

Monday, 1st March.—KURKARÍ BÉNT. 15½ miles.

Start southwards and make a slight detour to the left to regain the Bélá road. Here one comes somewhat abruptly on the scarp of the plateau. The track turns south-west and skirts it. On the right hand is a deep ravine, and its brink approaches in one place so close to the main scarp, that there is not more than 4 or 5 feet between them.

At 1¼ miles commenced the descent, which leads south-south-west down the face of the steep slope. It is rather a rough track at first, but about half-way down turns left (east) into the ravine between the scarp and a strangely placed outer ridge of bare rock, whose crest has been for a long way back visible over the gravel slopes. The latter part of the descent is good. Total fall about 250 feet in a quarter of a mile of road.

Having gained the ravine, proceed along it in an easterly direction. At 2 miles a more roundabout, but better, track comes in from the left. Heavy laden camels take this path.

The road turning east-south-east now passes through a gap in the ridge, and bending south-south-east leads down a small stony darah between plateaux of no great height. The watercourse, however, turns off to the right through low hills beyond the ridge.

At 3½ miles, having finally quitted the Bélá road, bend south and ascend to a gravel plateau sloping gently southwards.

Across this south-south-east, reaching at 4¾ miles the Lesser Wádí Nála which comes round from the right and run south-east. The surrounding country as far as the base of Drún is now seen to be low bare plateaux and small clayey hills. A headland of the high plateau from which we have descended is at some distance to the right.

Crossing the shallow watercourse the track leads south by east, and very soon descends under white clay hillocks to the Greater Wádí Nála, joined by another from the right. This is a good sized kaur of the usual type.

The track goes south-south-east under the clay scarp, and at 6¼ miles turns to left through low hillocks, the nála going south.

Wind through insignificant elevations, preserving the same general direction, and at 7¾ miles re-enter the Wádí, which has come round from the right. The road descends it, still keeping about south-south-east.

At 8¼ miles there is an eastward bend, but the old direction is soon resumed. A large nála here comes in from the right.

Crossing the mouth of this, and over a small bent, the Wádí is regained, at 9 miles, a short distance above its junction with the Arah Kaur, which comes from the north-east.

From thence take to the right bank, proceeding south-south-west parallel to the kaur, over light sandy soil, grown with scrub and tamarisk.

At 10¼ miles cross a small affluent nála. Thence south over the same sort of ground. Low hills on the right, kaur on the left.

At 10¾ miles a higher gravelly plateau is crossed south-south-east.

Thence descend at 11½ miles to soft ground and tamarisk jungle, and after a short distance enter the kaur, which has now a broad stony bed pretty thickly grown with tamarisk. It is flanked by low flats, and further off are small hills, mostly clayey.

Here, at 12 miles, is a small rainpool, the first water since leaving the Áoghání ravine. The place is called Dárí-é-Mand.

From thence descend the wide kaur. Its actual channel is stony, but there is also a fair amount of alluvium in its bed, and the road is good. Water in pools is met with every few hundred yards.

At about 13¾ miles the Kor-a-Kaur, running under Drún, joins from the right. There is plenty of wood, water, and camel grazing here, and apparently a good camping would not be very difficult to find. There is also grass. Troops would halt hereabouts, but we went on further to Kurkarí Bént. For about 4 miles down from Dárí-é-Mand one place is pretty much the same as another, and a halt may be made anywhere. The water is slightly saline and muddy, but drinkable enough. Some of the pools are very large, though not deep. Evidently there is more than mere rain water, and a supply may be counted on, except after several perfectly dry seasons.

At Kurkarí Bént one is well within the high hills, Drún towering on the right and Wáshapí on the left. The sandstone of which these remarkable hills are composed appears identical with that of the coast ranges. The road on to Drún is up a deep cleft immediately opposite to Kurkarí Bént.

Tuesday, 2nd March.—REGIWÁR. 12 miles. Elevation 610 feet.

Southwards, and soon after leaving camp ascend to a stony plateau under Drún on the right bank of the kaur.

After half a mile the track leads along the face of a very steep slope, with a fall of about 100 feet to the stony bed of the nála below. Thence across a small elevated plateau. The descent from this is rather rough in two or three short zigzags, and leads to a lower flat.

At $1\frac{1}{2}$ miles regain the kaur, now only 50 or 60 yards wide, winding between rather lofty plateaux which project from the base of the high cliffs on either side. There is abundant water here. It runs a little. The road is stony, but fair.

At $2\frac{1}{2}$ miles the kaur bends somewhat to the right (westwards), and there is a long straight reach. Here the track is good, over a low bent on the left bank. On the further side, the nála is bounded by a precipitous rock, broken in places, and forming the scarp of a high plateau under Drún.

At 3 miles, the bent having come to an end, the kaur is crossed diagonally, and the track leads over another bent, descending again to the nála bed at $3\frac{1}{2}$ miles. The latter is now followed for some little way, but at 4 miles the right bank is ascended. All these ascents and descents are slight and easy, unless otherwise mentioned.

At $4\frac{1}{2}$ miles the kaur is crossed, and the track turns south-east on the right bank. The nála here makes a decided bend to the east. The track, after going south-east, bends at first east, and then north-east, describing a semi-circle on a small stony plain called Bangí.

At 6 miles ascend to a stony irregular plateau, and at $6\frac{1}{4}$ miles climb to a higher step of the same. The track turning north, then gains the third and highest level at $6\frac{3}{4}$ miles.

This is a very narrow plateau, enclosed by a northerly loop of the kaur. From this point we obtained a view of the gap in the next high range to south, where we shall strike the Hingól river. It bore about south-west by south, and appeared only 15 miles distant, but is really more. The intervening country, as far as we could see it, is a wilderness of low clayey hills tossed in wild confusion around the course of the Arah Kaur which we are following. The general character of the whole of this region is strikingly different from that more to the west which we crossed between Urmára and the the Kólwáh plain at Chambúr.

The descent is south-south-east down the face of a very steep slope to the nála, about 240 feet below. The path is fairly good, but heavy laden camels would keep to the bed of the kaur, the additional distance being as nothing to these animals in comparison with the heavy gradients.

The nála when reached is crossed, and the track leads over a plateau of moderate height. Direction about south-south-west. The kaur now winds in a narrow valley bounded by low clayey hills, all scarped, those towards Drún being of fantastic shapes. The flats on either side of the watercourse are sometimes stony, but quite as often of good alluvial soil. The high hills now open out to right and left. On the one side an outer ridge of Wáshapí sinks to an insignificant elevation, but hides the main mass behind it. On the other, the strange, stair-like cliffs of Drún bend away westward.

The road lies along the left bank of the nála. At 8 miles passed a few huts at a spot called Búzí. Water in pools is everywhere abundant.

At $8\frac{3}{4}$ miles bend slightly round westwards. General direction south-east by south.

At 10 miles ascend to a bent on the right bank. At $10\frac{1}{2}$ miles, having regained the kaur, skirt the left bank for a short distance.

At 11 miles the valley is wider and partially wooded. It bends westwards towards Drún. About here there are some traces of cultivation on the right bank at a place called Haibúí Bént.

At about 11½ miles turn east-south-east, but at 12 miles again westward, and cross a bent. The kaur is soon met, running under small clayey hills with a scarped face. At the foot of these is a pool of tolerably good water, and we halted. This spot is called Regiwár. It is a favorite resting place, as the water below here is said to be very salt for a long way. Plenty of room to camp but the ground is rather stony. Water abundant; also wood and camel grazing. Some *gurkao* grass.

This march in point of time was as long as that of yesterday. Still there are really no difficulties.

Wednesday, 3rd March.—POLAL-A-BÉNT. 21 miles. Elevation 306 feet.

Crossed the nála diagonally; then over a plateau south-east by south, the kaur going in a deep bed to the right.

At 1½ miles crossed the channel. Thence south-west over an alluvial flat.

At 2 miles crossed again. Ground alluvial and stony. Direction south south-west.

After about half a mile again met the kaur under a clay cliff. Cross and turn west.

At 3¼ miles climb the side of a high plateau and turn along it south. At one point the bed of the nála is close below on the left. Thence an easy descent to a gravel and alluvial flat gained at 3¾ miles.

Here turn south-west. At 4 miles west-south-west. Gravel and alluvial flats, and road very good, but it is provoking to make so much westing when the direct course is nearly south.

At 4¾ miles west. The kaur is near at hand on the left.

At 5¼ miles pass the end of a small isolated clay hill. It is scarped on both sides, and the base appears to be but a few yards thick. There are hundreds such, but one of the most striking peculiarities of the strange little hills is seldom so observable.

Hence bend west by south. At 6½ miles enter the kaur, and pass along it westwards. The track is stony and sandy, and the bed of the watercourse is filled with old half dead tamarisk.

At 6¾ miles ascend the left bank, bending south-west, and gain (at 7 miles) a high plateau by an easy ascent.

Thence south-south-west. Gentle descent to an alluvial flat, and cross the kaur at 7½ miles. Beyond is another easy ascent to a stony plateau, on which the track turns west-south-west. Again a gentle descent to an alluvial flat.

At 8½ miles the kaur, and straight on over it. Easy ascent to a gravel plateau and turn south. Descend again gradually to an alluvial flat and turn south by east.

At 9½ miles cross the kaur, gaining right bank by a slight ascent. Thence pass over a small rise.

At 10 miles bend west, and shortly afterwards west by north across a wooded flat. The road so far is very good, but monotonous and uninteresting. The low clayey hills are continuous on either hand, enclosing a sort of valley, a mile or so wide, from side to side of which the nála winds, the road maintaining as straight a course as possible over the adjacent flats.

The kaur is now crossed from the right to the left bank; its bed is sandy. Then, at 11 miles, a stony flat, on which turn west by south. Here, however, are a few traces of cultivation. The place is known as Píroshí Bént. Thence west-south-west, bending west over a sandy flat with low scrub.

At 12 miles a nála from the left, which is crossed, and also the kaur; afterwards a stony flat with tamarisk jungle.

Thence cross the kaur diagonally westwards and turn south over a bent.

At 13 miles cross the kaur diagonally south by west, and ascend right bank to a stony flat, bending south-south-west.

At 13¾ miles ascend to a gravelly plateau, bending south through undulating stony ground, succeeded by a small stony plain surrounded by small elevations. The kaur is some distance on the left.

At 15 miles bend to the right through low hills, and after a slight ascent turn southwards. At 15¼ miles east-south-east, and descend a very narrow ravine winding south-east through low clayey hills.

At 15¾ miles turn to right (east) up a small side ravine to a watershed, thence turning south and quitting the hills almost immediately. Beyond them is the kaur 150 yards wide, and running from east to west. The track turns down it south-west.

At 17¼ miles is Shúré Áp. Water under a clay scarp on the right bank. Here is the ordinary halting place.

On the left is a stony plateau, which might make a camping ground, but there is probably a better place below, a little off the road. Wood, camel grazing, and *drab* grass abundant; also some *gurkao*.

Being anxious to reach the river, we pushed on, ascending the left bank of the watercourse, and turning south over stony ground. After a short distance bend south-east over alluvial flat. The kaur is now seen going away south by west.

The country is now more open. There are low hills in front, some of them rocky, and clay hills to the left up to the base of the high ranges here called Gúrángat. The track crosses an alluvial plain, with low scrub and scattered tamarisk, for about 1½ miles in a southerly direction.

Thence, ascending to a slightly higher level, it enters a stony and broken track, crossing some small watercourses. General direction somewhat east of south towards a small but conspicuous clay hill.

The base of this is reached at about 20¼ miles, and the track winds round its left, and turns west-south-west descending a shallow watercourse.

At 20¾ miles turn south and reach the left bank of the Hingól river (here commonly known as the *Mazand Kaur* (or " big nála"). It comes from north-west, and stretches away south to the high hills, now only a few miles off.

Where reached, the bank of the kaur is scarped, and one has to proceed a short distance further, making a slight detour to the left to avoid broken ground on the bank.

At about 21 miles, 3¾ miles from Shúré Áp, descended to the river and camped there under left bank. Wood, water, and camel grazing abundant. *Gurkao* grass on the hills. The best place for troops is probably on the right bank, which is more open than the left.

The bed of the kaur is about 200 yards broad, stony in some places, clayey and sandy in others, and well grown with tamarisk jungle. The banks, generally scarped, are 10 or 12 feet high. The running stream is neither large not swift. In places is spreads out to a considerable breadth. The water is sweet and good, but slightly muddy.

The name of this place is derived from the range to right (west) of the gorge, which is called Pohal.

Turning northwards the western half of Drún is seen to be much lower than the eastern under which we passed. The river comes round the west end, about west-north-west from here, and is somewhere there joined by the Párkíuí Kaur, which we crossed two marches south of Chambúr (11th February). There is a place in the low part of Drún called Rodén-i-Kachao, where there is a spring and some trees. There is generally a Bízanjáo camp about there, and the spring is well known as a watering place for flocks.

Ordered two sowars to start early to-morrow morning for Urmára to tell Basria Mal to send a boat round to Hingól.

There is a Bízanjáo camp on the kaur about a mile south-east.

The road to-day was good all the way.

Thursday, 4th March.—GWAND BENT. 8½ miles. Elevation 193 feet.

Start down the kaur southwards, inclining south-south-west. A good road through tamarisk jungle, but rather sandy.

At 1¼ miles enter the broad clear channel of the river, and turn down it south-east. After some distance the stream is crossed, and as the hills are entered, the road is rough, over large stones.

At about 3 miles one is fairly within the defile. The stream is now crossed again to the left bank.

Here it is shallow and stony, but immediately below commences to be deep and still, almost completely filling the bottom of the gorge.

At about 3¼ miles is a ford, 4 feet deep, and 25 yards across. The bottom is of firm sand, and camels cross without difficulty, as the current is almost imperceptible. A quarter of a mile lower down men can cross dry shod on boulders lying in the stream, but unfortunately a ledge of sandstone rock half way between this place and the ford bars the road to animals. Mules and ponies being taken up to this must be unloaded, taken round over the ford to the stepping stones, and brought up to the other side of the ledge, where they can be reloaded. The portage is therefore only a few yards over the rock, and a few sappers with dynamite would soon make a road through the obstacle. In its present condition the place altogether would considerably delay troops marching, and it is evident that a slight rise of the stream would render the ford impracticable to laden camels.

In going by the ford the pool is re-entered for a few yards to pass round a projecting rock corresponding to the ledge abovementioned. It is rather an awkward little bit.

Having got over to the other side of the stream, proceed down it along right bank, which slopes rather steeply to the water. The average breadth of the gorge is about 120 yards. The sides are high and inaccessible sandstone cliffs. In this defile floods rise to a height of 30 or 40 feet as evinced by drift wood on the banks. The guide informed us that about 4 years ago (1877) there was a remarkable flood, which, according to the marks he showed, must have been fully 50 feet above the ordinary level of the stream. The flood season is in June and July, as might be expected, but there is often some rain after Christmas.

At about 5 miles the defile bends quite round to east-south-east. The road, still keeping the right bank, is sometimes rough, but generally fair travelling. The hills are now lower, but equally inaccessible.

At 6½ miles the defile makes an abrupt turn to the left (south), and the stream is crossed. It is quite shallow.

At 7 miles the gorge is passed, and the road, crossing again, ascends to a wide bent on the right bank, cutting off an easterly sweep of the river.

At 8½ miles the river is again met and crossed. We camped here on the left bank. The flats on both sides are known as Gwand Bént. That just passed over would make a good camping ground. It is alluvial soil grown with low scrub. Wood and camel grazing abundant. Grass from the hills moderate.

The distance from Shúré Áp is about 12 miles.

This country belongs to Las Béla, the gorge just passed being the boundary. The river is called Hingól from the same place, or probably from the junction of the Arah Kaur.

Friday, 5th March.—ACHÓR. 13 miles. Elevation 38 feet.

From camp south-east towards a plateau on that side, and enter a ravine. A camel road goes on over the flat, but is longer. The track, winding through low clayey hills, ascends and descends slightly.

At ¾ of a mile strike the Sítal Nála, coming from between the high hills on the left. It is a small watercourse grown with tamarisk and grass, and is followed southwards for a quarter of a mile. Here the track bends south-south-west over a bent. There is water in the nála here, but it is salt.

At 1½ miles descend a bank and cross the Sítal, which goes away north-west flanked by a white clay scrap. Thence wind south through small clay hills, a furrowed cliff on the right.

At 2½ miles cross a watershed. The track is still southwards through a hillocky tract.

At 3½ miles bend south-west, and a quarter of a mile further turn again to south-east. Here is open country covered with bushes and a few small trees. The first range beyond Gúrángat, called Sítal-i-Band, is now close at hand on the left. A corresponding range known as Kúlf is some miles off on the right. Road and river pass southwards through the wide gap between these hills. The former keeps pretty close to the Sítal range, beyond which is a high scarped mass of sandstone called Drang, and passes through somewhat thick jungle.

At 5 miles reach the Pacharí Nála from between Sítal-i-Band and Drang. It is 80 or 100 yards across, and the banks are thickly wooded. The bed is quite dry, and mostly of red sand.

Crossing this kaur the track continues still southwards, through tamarisk jungle. At 5¾ miles it turns to the right, and descends to the sandy river bed, which is crossed diagonally (south-west.) The stream is here broad and shallow. Having gained the right bank, turn south along it through thick jungle.

At 7 miles again meet the river, which bends to the right, and turn down it west.

At 7½ miles turn south across a ford 15 yards wide and a foot deep. It has a firm sandy bottom. Thence southward through tamarisk jungle, the hills closing in on both sides.

At 8½ miles pass through a gap about 300 yards wide, skirting a yellow sandstone rock on the left.

At 9 miles the river, and along its sandy bed, still south.

At 9¼ miles cross the stream in two small shallow channels and ascend the right bank.

Thence bend south-west by south down a long and tolerably straight valley about a mile wide. On the right is a sandstone cliff; on the left a marvellously fissured clayey scarp. The flats on either side the river bed are thickly wooded with tamarisk, &c.

At 11 miles descend a scarped bank to the river (baggage animals had better keep to its bed), and cross an easy ford to a flat on the left bank.

At 11¾ miles again descend to the river. The ford here is pebbly. The track, on the right bank, now inclines towards the base of the rocks, and at about 12½ miles reaches the mouth of the Náni ravine. This is a large and deep cleft, about two miles up which is Hingláj or Bíbí Nání, a famous place of Hindu pilgrimage.

Crossing the woody watercourse as it issues from the hills, the track continues near the base of the cliff. At about 13 miles is a towering rock, perfectly perpendicular, and 400 feet high. At the foot of this we camped in thick tamarisk jungle. For a mile or more below the mouth of the Hingláj ravine, the valley is known as Aghór, and the cliff is the Aghór rock mentioned by Goldsmid.

The bed of the river is here a sheet of sand 150 yards wide. The stream varies from 15 to 40 yards across, and is generally shallow. The banks are 12 feet high and scarped. On the right bank there is no room for encampment, The flat on the left bank is more suitable, but some jungle would apparently have to be cleared. There is also room in the river bed, and it would probably be safe enough in the cold weather. However, the sand is almost too soft for pitching tents. Wood, water, and camel grazing are abundant. There is also coarse *drab* grass.

Saturday, 6th March.—HINGÓL. 11¼ miles.

Waited this morning to allow the Hindus of the party to visit Hingláj, which has been sufficiently described by Goldsmid.

Started about half past two. At this hour the sea breeze is in full blow, and the heat is not unpleasantly great, but the still mornings are oppressive.

Followed a track along right bank, which winds about through jungle and over somewhat broken ground at the base of the rocks. The guide said this was better than taking to the river bed at once.

At 1 mile descended to the river and followed its sandy bed south-west bending west-south-west. The road is heavy.

At 1¾ miles south-west across the stream, shallow and stony. The river here bends southwards through the hills, but straight on is a long vista through low parallel broken ridges of strange shaped rocks. A good deal of this country would afford a Doré valuable suggestions for illustrating "Paradise Lost," but *not* with reference to those passages treating of paradise.

At 2 miles turn south, the river running under clay hills to the right. At 2¼ miles pass under the telegraph wire, which makes a tremendous leap to a small rocky ridge on the far side the stream.

The gap in the clay hills is wide, and the track winds over high broken ground near the eastern scarp. General direction south-south-east.

At 2¾ miles descend through clay hills at the foot of the cliff. The path is smooth, but far from level.

At 3½ miles reach a narrow plain between the clay hills and the last range, which is of sandstone.

The telegraph line is seen coming over this plain from the south-east, and the Urmára road leads over it westwards.

Very soon the track turns to the right, and descends an almost perpendicular, but soft, bank to the river bed. The stream is at the foot of this, and the track runs along under the bank for 100 yards or so to get a good crossing.

Thence south by east down the river bed over rather heavy sand, turning south by east at 4½ miles.

At 4½ miles cross the stream and enter the gap in the last range by which the river escapes to the sea. This gap is about 150 yards wide. The rocks on either hand are of no great height, and are accessible from the south, though scarped to the north.

Passing here over a low flat on the left bank, the track soon takes again to the river bed, which is gravelly, and continues down it south by west. On both sides are insignificant sandstone ridges, parallel to the last range, and at right angles to the river.

At 5¼ miles turn to the right and cross the stream for the last time. The ford is at the lower end of a long pool, and is 30 yards wide by 18 inches deep. Good sandy bottom. Thence ascend right bank and turn along it south-south-west through grass and jungle.

At 5½ miles bend south-south-west through low sandstone hillocks. These are soon cleared, and the track turns south-west, outside of and parallel to them.

On the left (south) is a sandy, uneven plain grown with very low scrub and tufts of dead grass. Sand dunes similarly covered shut out a view of the sea, which is not, however, far off.

At 7½ miles reach outlying hillocks. Beyond these, at 7¾ miles, is the shallow sandy bed of the Malí Nála, in which some babul and tamarisks have been conspicuous objects since leaving the hills.

Thence over the same plain bending somewhat to the south. The travelling is good, but there is no defined track.

At 10 miles rise slightly on to sand dunes with low scrub, from the top of which, at 10¼ miles, a glimpse of the sea is obtained. Descend slightly therefrom, and cross a portion of the plain towards more sand dunes. Near these (11¼ miles) came suddenly on a well, and were surprised to hear we were at Hingól, as I had expected a village or visible hamlet of some sort. There are however, only some ten or a dozen widely scattered fishermen's huts.

Camped at the well. Soil very sandy, and almost too loose for pitching tents. It is covered with low scrub, and there is tamarisk, so camel grazing and wood are fairly plentiful. The water in this well is scanty, and rather brackish, but three-quarters of a mile west, across heavy sand, is another. The water in this is quite near the surface and perfectly sweet, so that there can be little doubt it is a spring, and not infiltrated sea water.

The sandstone range last traversed, and its accompanying outer ridges, run straight about south-west, and passing a little north of the wells, terminate in the sea some two miles west-south-west. They are locally known as Hab. The point is apparently that next to Málán on the east, but the latter is 12 or 15 miles off.

The sea is a short mile south of the wells. It is very shallow and full of sand banks. There is deeper water off the point, but, as far as I could ascertain, steamers would have to anchor a long way out in a perfectly open roadstead.

Sunday, 7th March.—Halted. Owing to impossibility of obtaining even the smallest amount of supplies (except fish and mutton) was obliged to send the party to Sangal, a march on the Suumiáni road, where there is a bannia's shop. The Rasaldar and two men, without their mares, elected to stay with me and go by boat to Karáchí.

It is hardly necessary to remark that there is no trade at Hingól, and in fact no boats larger than "yákdárs" (tonies or fishing canoes). A few camels come down occasionally from the interior to the mouth of the Hingól river for salt.

Monday, 8th March.—The boat from Urmára came in about midday. Though only a coasting craft of about 20 tons, the nákhuda did not care to come within half a mile of the land, abreast of the point.

We packed up leisurely, and embarked in tonies from the beach, under the rocks, about 1¼ miles south-west of our camp at the brackish well.

At about six we were under weigh, standing out very slowly with the beginning of the land breeze.

Tuesday, 9th March.—Ran steadily all night before a gentle land breeze, and about 6 A.M. sighted Churnáo island. The wind falling very light, we were not abreast till 11-30. Cape Monze of the charts is a range running apparently parallel to the shore but its strike is probably north east. Its local, and presumably correct, name is *Jil*, "Monze" and "Muárí" being unknown to the boatmen.

At 4 o'clock we were off Manora, and landed at the custom-house bunder about 5, thus terminating the expedition.

The distance by sea from Karáchí harbour to Hingól anchorage is about 105 miles.

The following is a list of words occasionally used in the foregoing pages, or which might be useful to a future traveller as being of constant occurrence:—

Band.—Commonly applied to a range of hills in Mekrán.

Bént.—A plateau; more especially a plateau abutting on, or enclosed by the bend of, a watercourse.

Bidrang.—Watershed.

Bunáp.—Water which wells up from below in contradistinction to rain water. Answers to the 'sim' of eastern Balúchistán and Sind.

Bút.—A spur (Balúchí).

Búz.—A spur (Bráhúí).

Cháh.—Well.

Daf.—Mouth, as of a stream or ravine.

Dák.—Clear plain.

Dámán.—Literally *skirt*; it means the stony glacís, or foot slope of a hill.

Damók.—A narrow plain or valley with parallel ranges on either hand.—(*Ross*).

Dár.—Wood.

Dát.—Cliff; also a place enclosed by cliffs, *i.e.*, a ravine or defile.

Dhán.—Waste or desert.

Ghidán.—The common black blanket tent of the country.

Halk.—See Tuman.

Hor.—Literally finger; sometimes applied to peaks.

Kalát, or Kalag.—A fort.

Kand.—A pass; answers to "kotal."

Káuí.—A waterhole.

Kaur.—Watercourse; answers to the Indian ' nála.'

Khushkáwa.—Land dependent on rain.

Koh.—It is hardly necessary to mention that this word means mountain.

Kohán.—A peak.

Kúcha.—A plain.

Lak.—A pass; answers nearly to the Indian 'ghat,' and seems to imply a place of which the ascent is much greater on one side than the other. It is not, I believe, a Balúch or Persian word.

Lat.—A range of hills (Bráhúí).

Mach.—A date tree.

Mánchar or Mántar.—A loop or bend, as of a stream; also circuitous, as of a road.

Marao.—Topographically a basin—*i.e.*, a place the drainage of which has no outlet, and which is therefore liable to become flooded after rain.

Reg, or rek.—Sand; also a sandhill.

Rém.—Grass.

Sim.—See Bunáp.

Sor.—Salt; answers to "shor."

Sunt.—An end; applied to the termination of a range or of a spur.

Tank.—A defile; answers to " tangi."

Takar.—Literally hill or rock. It also means everywhere a section of a tribe.

Tálár.—Steep or inaccessible.

Thal.—Sometimes small plains of alluvial soil are found high up among the hills. In a less dry climate these would be lakes or tarns. Such places are called *thal*.

Thúl.—A tower.

Tuman.—A camp or collection of ghidáns. In Mekrán it is *halk*.

Zíarát.—Shrine; the burial-place of a saint.

Six well known kinds of grass are met with, it is useful to know their names and quality.

Good prickly grass is *kándár* or kándéra	1
A fine soft hill grass is *pítár*—good	2
Rather coarse but abundant hill grass is *gurkao*	3
Common grass in the plains in *barshón*	4
Grass growing in tussocks on plains, &c., is *drab* or *kán*	5
Grass growing in tussocks in watercourses, &c., is *kásham*	6

No. 1 is more common about hollows of hills than anywhere else. It is killed by frost and then is of no use. When green, horses eat it greedily.

No. 2 is a good grass and abundant in some places.

No. 3 is also good and abundant on nearly all hills.

No. 4 is tolerable. The old stuff is like sticks.

No. 5 horses will eat from hunger, but not willingly.

No. 6 hardly as good as No 5.

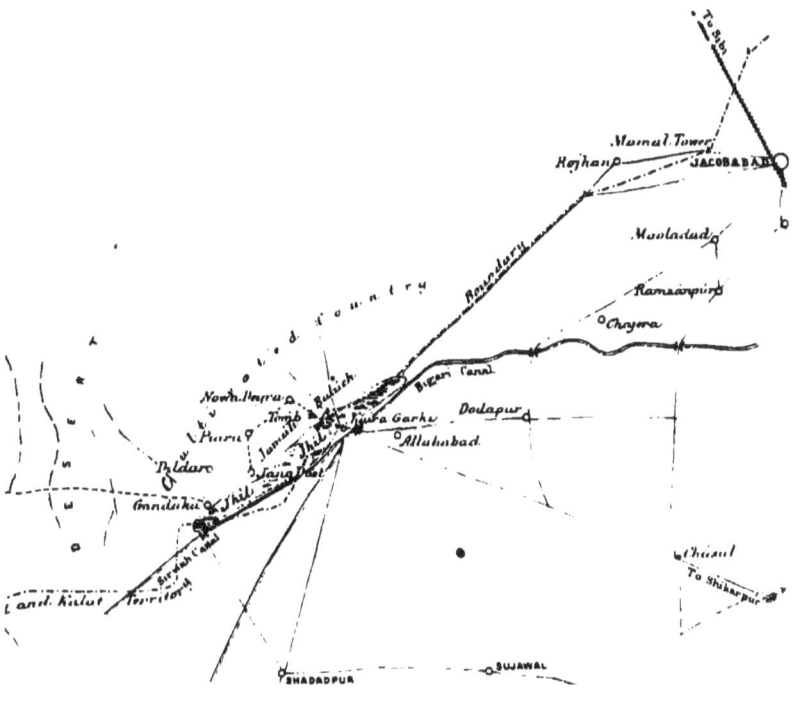

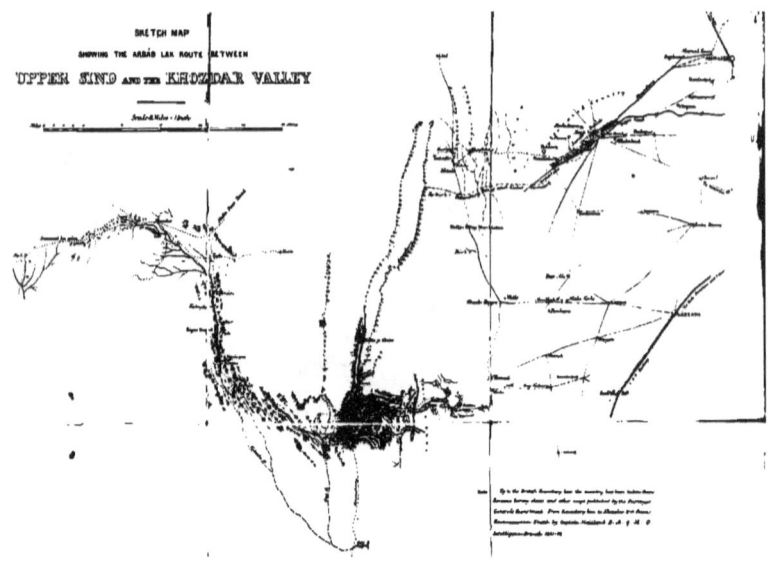

www.ingramcontent.com/pod-product-compliance
Lightning Source LLC
Chambersburg PA
CBHW030408170426
43202CB00010B/1533